PUNK
THE BRUTAL TRUTH

Publisher and Creative Director: Nick Wells
Project Editor and Picture Research: Sara Robson
Art Director and Layout Design: Mike Spender
Digital Design and Production: Chris Herbert

Special thanks to: Laura Bulbeck, Helen Crust, Anna Groves, Amanda Leigh, Geoffrey Meadon and Polly Prior

First published 2012 by
FLAME TREE PUBLISHING
Crabtree Hall, Crabtree Lane
Fulham, London SW6 6TY
United Kingdom

www.flametreepublishing.com
Music information site: www.flametreemusic.com

© 2012 Flame Tree Publishing Ltd

12 14 16 15 13
1 3 5 7 9 8 6 4 2

The CIP record for this book is available from the British Library.

ISBN: 978-0-85775-400-4

HUGH FIELDER (Author)

Hugh Fielder was news editor at *Sounds* – the first rock weekly to cover the punk scene – in 1976. As a child of the 1960s, punk rattled his hippy ideals but after seeing The Ramones at London's Roundhouse he was easily converted. He was present when the paper replaced Rod Stewart on the cover with The Damned – a seminal moment. He watched punk writer Jane Suck throw a typewriter out of the office window and Oi band Cockney Rejects beat up the features editor. He was also the recipient of one (used) boot and a pair of crotchless panties from Ian Dury's press officer and a peck on the cheek from Debbie Harry when she came by the office one afternoon. The cheek has barely been washed since.

MIKE GENT (Author)

Nurturing an obsession with pop music which dates back to first hearing Slade's 'Gudbuy T'Jane' in 1972, Mike Gent remains fixated, despite failing to master any musical instrument, with the possible exception of the recorder. A freelance writer since 2001, he has contributed to *Writers' Forum, Book and Magazine Collector, Record Buyer, When Saturday Comes, Inside David Bowie and the Spiders* (DVD), *The Kinks 1964–1978* (DVD), *The Beatles 1962–1970* (DVD), *Remember the Eighties, Where Were You When? – Music That Changed Our Lives, The Definitive Illustrated Encyclopedia of Rock* and *The Little Book of the World Cup*.

PAUL DU NOYER (Introduction)

Paul Du Noyer began his career on the *New Musical Express* then went on to edit *Q* and to found *Mojo*. He also helped to launch *Heat* and several music websites. As well as editing several rock reference books, he is the author of *We All Shine On*, about the solo music of John Lennon, and *Wondrous Place*, a history of the Liverpool music scene. He is nowadays a contributing editor of *The Word*.

Picture Credits

Printed in China

PUNK
THE BRUTAL TRUTH

BY HUGH FIELDER AND MIKE GENT

INTRODUCTION BY PAUL DU NOYER

FLAME TREE
PUBLISHING

CONTENTS

THE AFTERMATH: 1979 & BEYOND 144

INTRODUCTION

In our heads we can all imagine a noise called punk rock. It's nasty, brutish and short. It's played on cheap guitars at high speed. In fact it's possibly played *on* cheap speed. The songs are basic to the point of wilful stupidity. If they have any message, it will probably be negative. The general effect will not be pretty or romantic. It might even be downright ugly.

And yet this noise will also be ridiculously exciting. Rarely in music has so much been achieved with so little. ('Here's one chord, here's another, now start a band,' said a fanzine.) The genre that liked to boast of its incompetence and loudly proclaim 'No Future' has turned out to be extremely enduring and long-lasting. Its surviving pioneers have lived to a ripe old age. Some of them go on TV to advertise butter, or car insurance. How the hell did that happen?

So let's take a closer look. For many, the classic punk event will always be The Sex Pistols. Circa 1976 and 1977, they defined the look of punk for all time. Their cut-up aesthetic perfectly captured their chaotic ideology. Its mix of anarchy and commercial opportunism was a barbed-wire bundle of contradictions, caught between a warring band and its management. Others will cite The Clash, who were the ultimate flag-wavers of punk idealism, brought low by contradictions of their own. They never quite reconciled the purity of their image with the realities of global success.

And others would probably point to The Ramones, a New York act who inspired the British scene into being and whose stripped-down musical minimalism remains the essence of the genre. Like Motörhead, a band from the neighbouring territory of hard rock, The Ramones endure as an iconic name, whose logo alone can sell a million T-shirts because it represents an attitude to life.

Yet, as this book seeks to prove, not even The Pistols, Clash and Ramones can encompass the whole of punk. The mid-1970s were pivotal to punk and New York and London were

its nerve centres, but this was a movement with numerous precedents and many influences. At its peak it would mutate into amazingly diverse forms, and later submerge and resurface, undergo profound changes and periodically purge itself in a return to first principles.

Punk is not limited to one particular place or time, because punk is really an idea. More than that, punk is an ideal, an urge, an instinct. For those reasons its followers can become passionate on the subject. For them, punk will always be much more than a style.

Punk is certainly more than a musical style. From the beginning it had parallels in fashion and graphic design. Since then it's shown a gift for shape-shifting that lives up to one of its earliest maxims: don't be content to imitate, go out and re-invent. Down the decades, punk has multiplied in form and merged with types of music that were once supposed to be its deadliest enemies, such as disco or avant-garde, or even – as The Pogues so powerfully demonstrated – the traditional Irish folk song.

A classical musician, Nigel Kennedy, can be a 'punk violinist'. Within weeks of punk rock erupting, there were punk poets led by John Cooper Clarke. Modern dance acquired its own punk figurehead in Michael Clark. There have been trends with names like punk-funk, steampunk and cowpunk. There was even a magazine called *Golf Punk*.

Early punk was all about simplicity, but not self-limitation. Punk rock musicians never cared much for musical proficiency. But they were musicians, despite themselves, and they grew

better at what they did. Healthy curiosity led them even further. While nothing beats the raw thrill of a three-chord bash, any true musician, even the punk rocker, has an imagination to satisfy. By a great irony, this proudly unprofessional school of musicianship has nurtured innovation and progress.

The first punk surge subsided, not because of apathy, but because its prime movers were artistically restless and wanted fresh fields to conquer. When the clubs filled up with copycat punkers who played to a formula, the genuine players regarded punk as a concept and not a template. Whether we call them post-punk or new wave, the next developments were not a watering-down of punk or – at least, not always – a calculated sell-out to chart acceptability. Punk at its best was a period of creative confusion, from which astonishing things could grow.

Punk does this. It is by its nature disruptive. It creates excitement, produces heat and promotes disturbance. Punk takes traditional elements and disorganizes them.

Punk values energy over expertise, but it values communication over both of those things. Punk values sincerity over eloquence, but it cannot bear to be boring. And deep inside every punk act, there is a subversive sense of humour. In all these ways, punk avoided becoming a creative dead-end.

As with all forms of rock, the early punk performers were usually male, but rarely macho. A movement that owes a large part of its being to Patti Smith was scornful of standard rock-god swaggering, and soon produced outstanding female acts like The Slits, Gaye Advert and Pauline Murray, alongside mainstream stars such as Debbie Harry and Chrissie Hynde. Punk is hardly known for celebrating sex or glamour (though it did have male pin-ups of a kind in Billy Idol and The Clash's Paul Simonon). The glory of punk was its respect for individuality. No stylist or public relations guru could have invented Johnny Rotten or Poly Styrene.

Before I'd heard of The Sex Pistols I knew a mad clothes shop in Chelsea. One day I saw a sign in the window that said 'New band. No flares. No cripples. Ask for Sid Vicious.' I don't know if anyone answered it. I know I didn't. In that summer of 1976 it was scary enough just going into Malcolm McLaren and Vivienne Westwood's shop, Sex. But that's where it all began and Sex gave birth to British punk.

Around the same time I stumbled upon a Sex Pistols show at the 100 Club in central London. It was obvious that something strange and possibly revolutionary was at hand, but as yet it had no label. None of us in the hot, cramped basement could really grasp what we were watching. I once saw a newsreel of the young Elvis Presley, sexy and outrageous, and his audience were laughing – actually laughing – because they hadn't yet learned what rock'n'roll was supposed to be. So it was with those Sex Pistols shows. Some laughed, some fled. Most of us just stood there, transfixed, fascinated. And the next week I came back for more.

And this became punk rock, something uniquely British, but with a debt to many things, from Little Richard to 1960s garage bands, to Bowie and his allies Iggy Pop and Lou Reed, and to the arty underground scene still thriving in New York. Nearly all rock is based upon some sort of rebellion, but punk was the first internal rebellion against rock itself. The Sex Pistols, The Damned and The Clash were not simply the next big thing. They were cultural revolutionaries who declared war on the rock establishment.

The Rolling Stones, Rod Stewart and Eric Clapton were singled out for contempt, along with hippy bands and prog-rockers. But none of those enemies ever disappeared, and the 'dinosaur' acts continued to rule. The only real victims of punk rock were the young, emerging acts who didn't quite fit the bill; and the biggest beneficiaries were slightly older acts – shrewd operators such as The Stranglers, Blondie and The Police – who were close enough to pass themselves off as punk, but also had the talent to touch on the mainstream.

In fact, once punk grew out of its early, snarling phase, it quickly broadened its appeal and joined the other pop trends of its time. By lowering the barriers to entry, punk liberated raw talents that might otherwise have gone unheard, such as Buzzcocks, The Undertones and Joy Division. By abolishing conventional standards of glamour, it raised the wire for some invaluable misfits to scramble underneath: Elvis Costello, Ian Dury and Squeeze. Then the self-destructive Sid Vicious finally succeeded in February 1979, and the first punk era was over.

But you could look around and see John Lydon's new band Public Image Ltd, or the Gang Of Four or the 2-Tone label, and sense that punk was fiercely alive in spirit, adopting fresh ideas and striking new alliances. We can see how punk regained its purism in Crass, fed the intensity of Nirvana, gave an edge to Britpop or found itself a youthful new voice in acts like Green Day. Its aftershocks have never really stopped.

This book shows that punk was not one-dimensional. Some ideas are so good they occur to more than one person at the same time. Punk was that kind of idea. And some ideas are so good that they keep coming back. Again, that's punk. Maybe every generation needs a punk moment. Let *Punk: The Brutal Truth* be your inspiration.

EARLY HISTORY: 1969-75

1969–75

Punk rock is about attitude more than music. It's not about how well you can play, it's about how well you can communicate. Its roots go back to the beginning of rock'n'roll in the 1950s. The rebellious spirit of MC5 and The Stooges in the 1960s helped to define the punk attitude, while Velvet Underground singer Lou Reed and the sleazy glam of The New York Dolls put flesh on punk's bones in the early 1970s.

The American punk scene developed around New York clubs like Max's Kansas City and CBGBs in the mid-1970s, where The Heartbreakers, Television and The Ramones all played, bands who would become the iconic sight and sound of punk rock.

In Britain it was the defiant stance of 1960s bands like The Who and The Small Faces that inspired a new generation of hard-edged R&B bands in the 1970s, such as Dr Feelgood and Eddie & The Hot Rods. But it was Malcolm McLaren who made the connection between the punk scene that had excited him in New York and the bunch of disaffected kids who were hanging around his fashion boutique in London's Kings Road. Once he'd found them a singer who was re-named Johnny Rotten, The Sex Pistols were born.

PROLOGUE

AMERICAN PUNK ROOTS

The roots of punk lie in rock'n'roll, itself a rebellious spin-off from rhythm and blues. 'Louie Louie', written by Richard Berry in 1955 and a US No. 2 hit for The Kingsmen in 1963, is often cited as the first punk song with its raw sound and almost indecipherable lyrics (nonetheless investigated by the FBI for obscenity). The song was covered by American garage bands like The Wailers and The Sonics (pictured opposite), as well as British beat groups like The Kinks and The Troggs. These bands all influenced the punk movement along with The Who, The Small Faces, The Velvet Underground, Love and psychedelic West Coast bands like The Seeds, Blue Cheer and Question Mark & The Mysterians.

1969

FEBRUARY

MC5 KICK OUT THE JAMS

Often credited as the first intentionally punk band, MC5's live debut album detonated in 1969. Forming at their Michigan High School, singer Rob Tyner, guitarists Wayne Kramer and Fred 'Sonic' Smith, bassist Michael Davis and drummer Dennis Thompson were mentored by political activist John Sinclair of The White Panthers. They were loud and brash and their lyrics had an incendiary edge. KICK OUT THE JAMS (a taunt they used to hurl at visiting laid-back West Coast bands), recorded in front of their Detroit home crowd, is fast, furious but focussed. Elektra Records managed to keep the word 'Motherf***ers' out of the title but left it on the record to the outrage of middle America.

AUGUST

THE STOOGES WANNA BE YOUR DOG

Hard on the heels of MC5 came fellow Detroit scoundrels The Stooges, fronted by trailer-park-trash singer James Osterberg (a.k.a. Iggy Pop, pictured left), who was prone to all manner of attention-seeking self-abuse off- and particularly on-stage. Their self-titled debut album had an equally abrasive raw power but producer John Cale of The Velvet Underground managed to strip the aural assault back to its essence. Meanwhile the lyrics eschewed the political in favour of the defiantly personal. The album made little impact at the time but both 'I Wanna Be Your Dog' and 'No Fun' are seminal punk classics containing all the vital ingredients.

1973

ALL DOLLED UP IN NEW YORK

Throwing a fistful of glitter into the mix, along with some debilitating drug problems, The New York Dolls (pictured opposite) tottered unsteadily along the line between punk and glam rock in the early 1970s. Fronted by the pouting Jagger-esque David Johansen, the band lost drummer Billy Murcia to a drug overdose before their self-titled first album in 1973. Inside their heads they were already stars and they galvanized the New York underground scene and the rock critics. But while they had a couple of sure-fire punk classics like 'Looking For A Kiss' and the aptly titled 'Personality Crisis', they had difficulty getting their act together in the studio.

1974

SPRING

THE NEW YORK SCENE

By the mid-1970s, the New York punk/new wave scene was starting to bubble. Acts like Patti Smith, Television and Talking Heads were emerging from the city's bohemian underground, alongside newly formed bands like The Ramones, Blondie, Wayne County, Johnny Thunders and Tuff Darts. The scene was centred around two clubs. Max's Kansas City, which had been one of The Velvet Underground's haunts, was immortalized in Lou Reed's 'Walk On The Wild Side' and Debbie Harry was a waitress there. The other was CBGBs, a run-down bar when Television first played there in the spring of 1974. Within a year CBGBs was the acknowledged home of New York punk. Even the sacred institution of marriage was not safe from punk's influence as wedding guests The Runaways' Joan Jett, Blondie's Debbie Harry, The New York Dolls' David Johansen and The Ramones' Joey Ramone (pictured) demonstrate.

JUNE

PATTI SMITH MAKES PUNK FROM POETRY

First of the New York crowd to get a record out was Patti Smith, a poet and writer who teamed up with guitarist and writer Lenny Kaye and pianist Richard Sohl to press their own single in the summer of 1974. It featured a taut, edgy version of 'Hey Joe' on one side and a poem about Patti's work experience in New Jersey, called 'Piss Factory', on the other. After a trip to California later that year, where the laid-back West Coast crowd was unimpressed by Patti's punk attitude and atonal rock poetry, they decided to up the ante and expand into a proper rock band – The Patti Smith Group.

AUGUST

THE RAMONES' FAMILY-STYLE PUNK

Forming at their Forest Hill High School in 1974, The Ramones quickly became the iconic sight and sound of punk rock. Singer Joey, guitarist Johnny, bassist Dee Dee and drummer Tommy shared the same surname and dress code: torn jeans and leather jackets. They played their first gig at CBGBs in August 1974 and gained an immediate residency, appearing 74 times before the end of the year, establishing their reputation with their 20-minute sets of two-minute songs, each counted in with a rapid 'one-two-three-four'. The songs – a wall of guitar chords, deadpan cartoon lyrics and no solos – reflected the underbelly of the Bowery where The Ramones hung out.

THE RAMONES

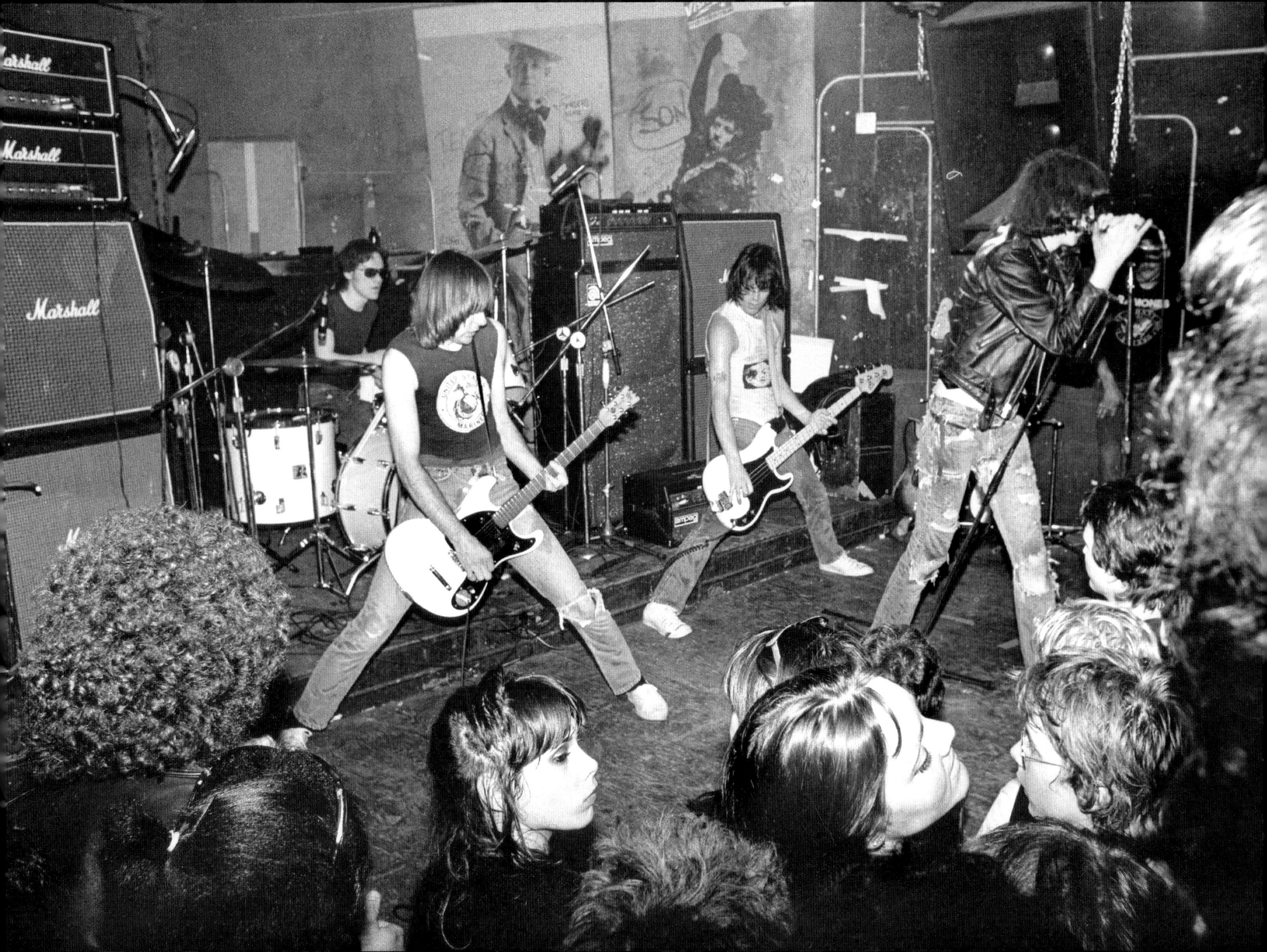

THE RAMONES

1975

MARCH

THE DICTATORS GO GIRL CRAZY

The anarchic Dictators spiced up the New York scene with their **GO GIRL CRAZY!** album in 1975, a coarse blend of punk and heavy metal with sharp witty lyrics mocking the junk culture they saw all around them, which naturally included punk and heavy metal. Unfortunately the chaos that surrounded the band meant that audiences were often bemused rather than amused by singer 'Handsome' Dick Manitoba and his slapstick sense of humour on songs like '(I Live For) Cars And Girls', 'The Next Big Thing' and 'Two Tub Man'. Besides which, punks were not ready for parody and humour; punk was still a serious thing.

MAY

TELEVISION'S LITTLE JEWEL

A volatile mixture of Tom Verlaine's taut, incisive guitar playing and bassist Richard Hell's avowedly punk attitude, Television were critically acclaimed from the moment they opened CBGBs as a punk rock venue in 1974. But the two styles proved incompatible and, during the ensuing power struggle in the spring of 1975, Hell found himself replaced by former MC5 bassist Fred 'Sonic' Smith. In August of that year they released the seven-minute 'Little Johnny Jewel' that was spread across both sides of a single – a tense, sparse, rhythmic song built around a simple riff that occasionally veered towards free-form jazz. Another punk possibility was opening up.

MAY

FROM DOLLS TO HEARTBREAKERS

As The New York Dolls subsided into a morass of conflicting visions and narcotic delusions in the spring of 1975, guitarist Johnny Thunders and drummer Jerry Nolan sealed the band's demise by suddenly bailing out to form The Heartbreakers (pictured above). They ditched the lip-gloss and donned the full punk leather jacket with ripped jeans, and they were joined by Richard Hell who had been drummed out of Television the very same week. With their previous connections they had a ready-made following and they soon built up a repertoire of hardcore songs, including the anthemic, none-too-subtly titled 'Chinese Rocks' co-written by Hell and Dee Dee Ramone.

THE NEW YORK SCENE HOTS UP

As the New York punk scene expanded, new bands began emerging. CBGBs waitress (and one-time Playboy bunny) Debbie Harry formed The Stilettos with a couple of girlfriends, and then Blondie with her boyfriend Chris Stein. Art school students David Byrne, Chris Frantz and his girlfriend Tina Weymouth put Talking Heads together. Tuff Darts were among the early frontrunners at CBGBs, with The Shirts and The Misfits not far behind. Others found that the punk umbrella suited their own eclectic style, like electronic duo Suicide, Willy Deville (pictured opposite) with his band Mink Deville, Wayne County & The Electric Chairs and Cherry Vanilla.

BRITISH PUNK ROOTS

British teenagers in the mid-1970s had little affinity with the overblown, so-called progressive bands that had come out of the 1960s. Glam rock had looked promising but there was little sense of rebellion beneath the make-up. Disaffected kids began looking for something that would reflect their own energies and frustrations. For a while it seemed as though the pub-rock scene and a new wave of Essex bands like Dr Feelgood (pictured opposite) and Eddie & The Hot Rods who were playing reinvigorated R&B might provide the answer. But whichever way you played it, R&B was still regarded as old-fashioned and the pub-rock scene was full of older musicians.

MAY

McLAREN PULLS THE TRIGGER WITH THE SEX PISTOLS

The British punk movement can be said to start with three West London teenagers hanging around a fashion boutique on the Kings Road called Sex, run by Malcolm McLaren and Vivienne Westwood, who had recently revamped the shop with a range of bondage, fetish and biker clothes. Despite their limited musical knowledge, Steve Jones, Paul Cook and Glen Matlock decided to form a band and learned to play bad covers of Faces and Bad Company songs. That was until McLaren returned from New York in May 1975 where he'd seen the excitement of the punk scene. He decided the three boys would make a perfect punk band. He altered their listening habits to include The Stooges and The New York Dolls, and found them a singer, a sneering North London kid called John Lydon, who was re-christened 'Johnny Rotten'. Just before their first gig, McLaren christened the band The Sex Pistols.

NOVEMBER

PATTI SMITH'S HORSES

The New York punk scene finally acquired a visible profile when Patti Smith signed to the prestigious Arista Records and released her first album in November 1975 titled **HORSES**. Produced by John Cale of The Velvet Underground, who knew a thing or two about the New York underground, the album catches the visceral dynamic between Patti's poetry and her band's raw, sparse sound. With her opening declaration that 'Jesus died for somebody's sins but not mine', Patti nailed her colours to the mast before proceeding to sample Van Morrison's Them classic for her own ends. It was a clear statement of intent.

LATE

THE RAMONES SIGN ON

Journalist Danny Fields took his friend Linda Stein to see The Ramones at CBGBs. Stein was married to Seymour Stein who had co-founded Sire Records, a label that specialized in releasing records by progressive British bands in America. Linda was smitten by The Ramones and persuaded her husband and Sire's A&R chief Craig Leon to come and see them. Leon could see the potential but had to work hard to convince Seymour. He also had to work on The Ramones who were looking for a bigger label. But when their demo tape was rejected by every company they had sent it to, they signed to Sire, and a couple of months later Linda and Danny started co-managing the band.

DECEMBER

PUNK MAGAZINE LAUNCHES

The New York punk scene finally got its own dedicated magazine at the end of 1975, when *Punk* was launched. It was set up by cartoonist John Holmstrom, who had previously worked for *Mad* magazine, 'resident punk' Eddie 'Legs' McNeil and publisher Ged Dunn, who had the money to finance it. The magazine popularized the punk scene in general and CBGBs in particular and early covers featured The Sex Pistols, Iggy Pop, Lou Reed, Blondie and The Ramones. The magazine also encouraged contributions from female writers and photographers, who were largely excluded from the male-dominated publishing world. This photograph of Joey Ramone and Debbie Harry posing for *Punk* magazine was taken by legendary punk photographer Roberta Bayley.

THE FIRST WAVE: 1976

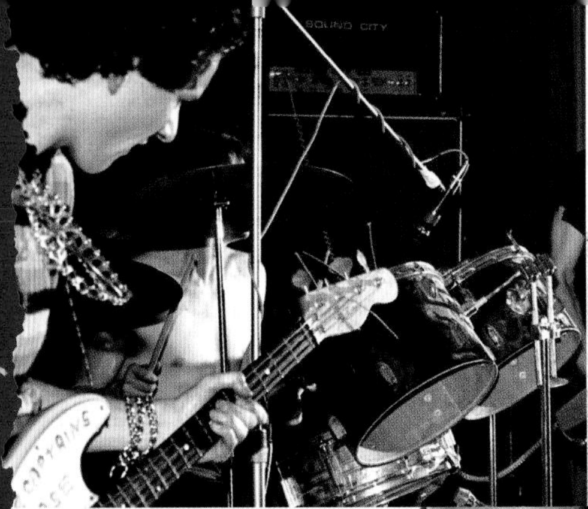
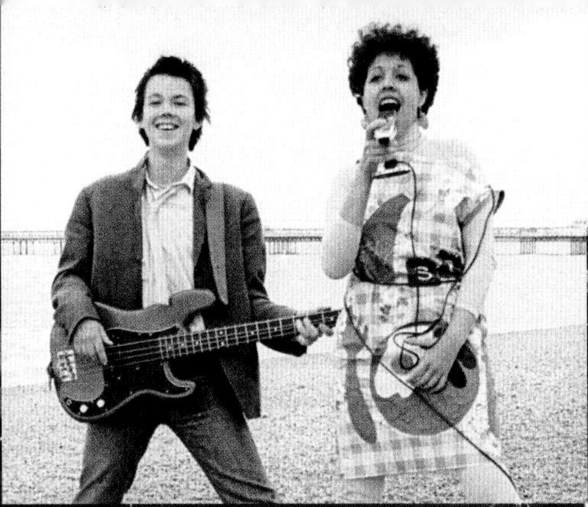
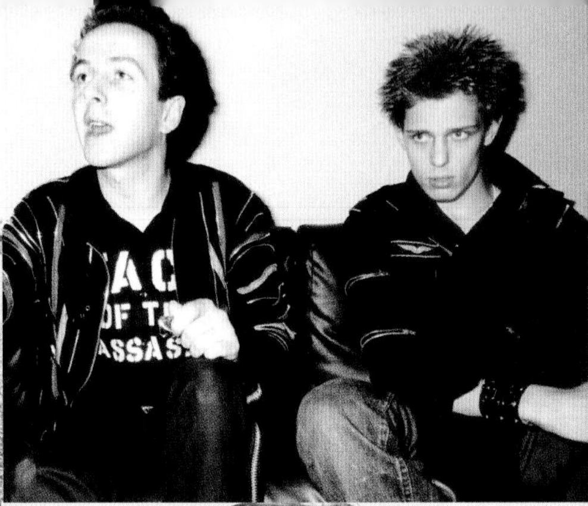
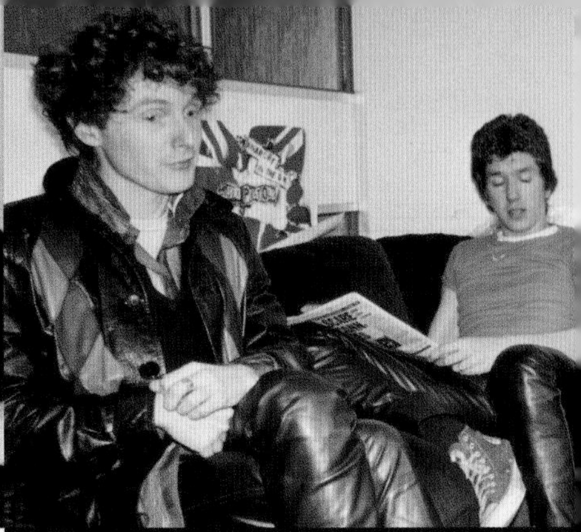
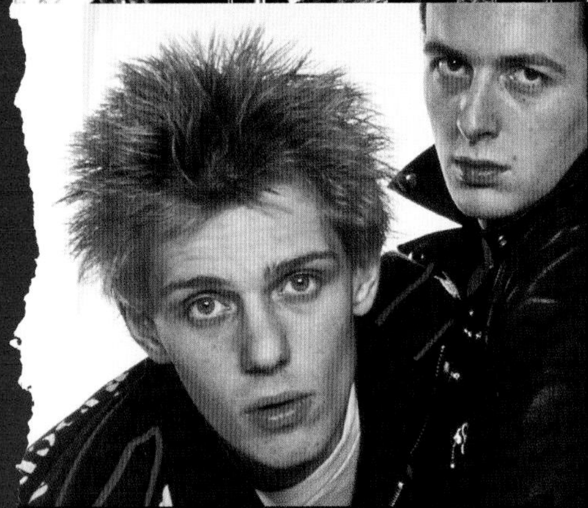
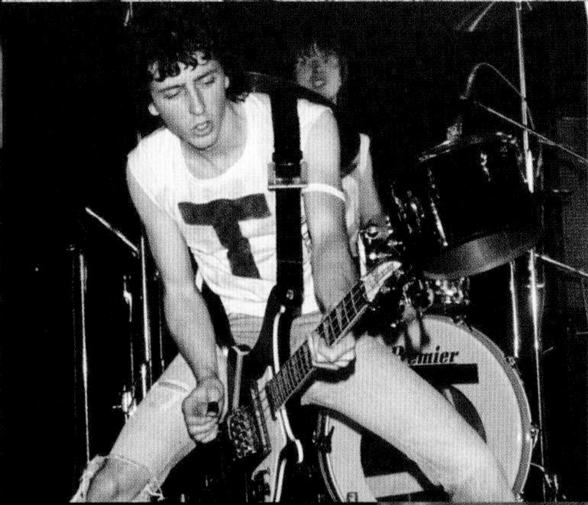
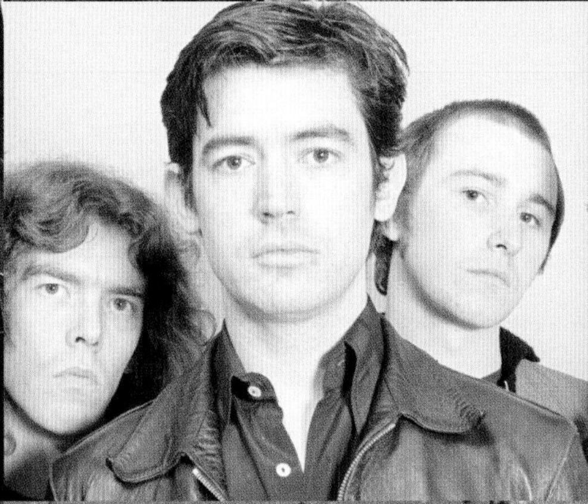
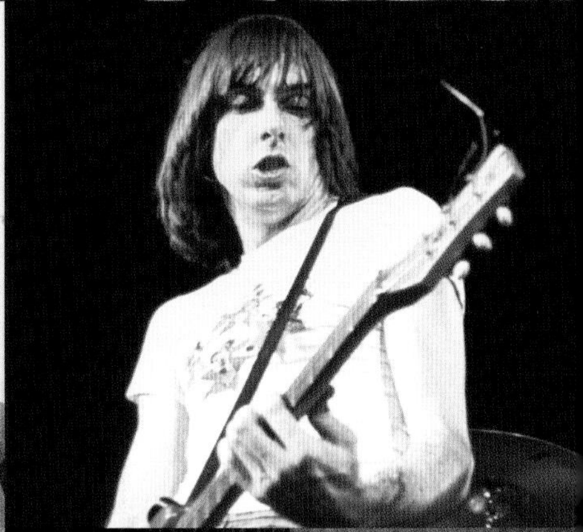
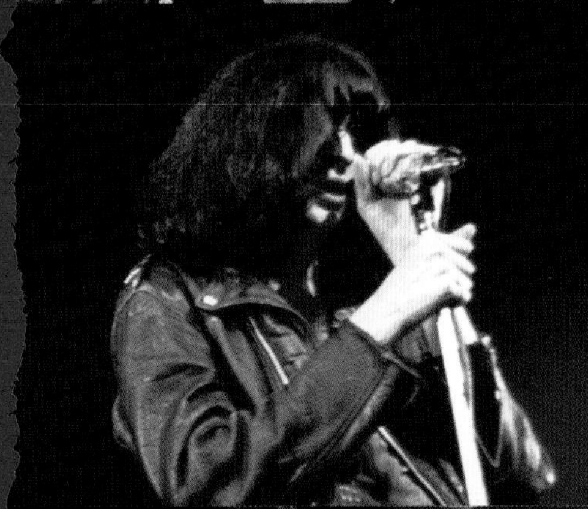
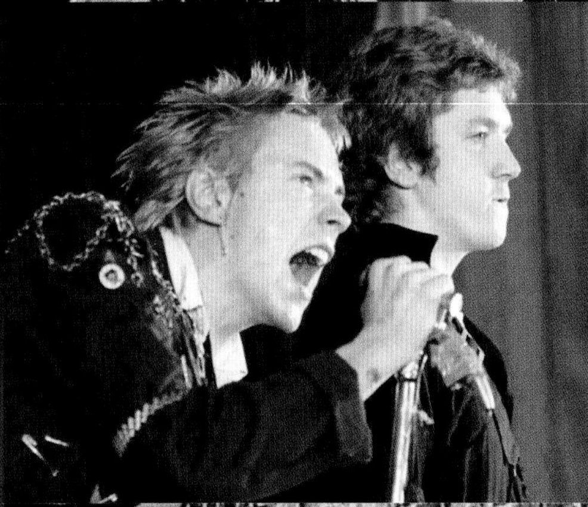
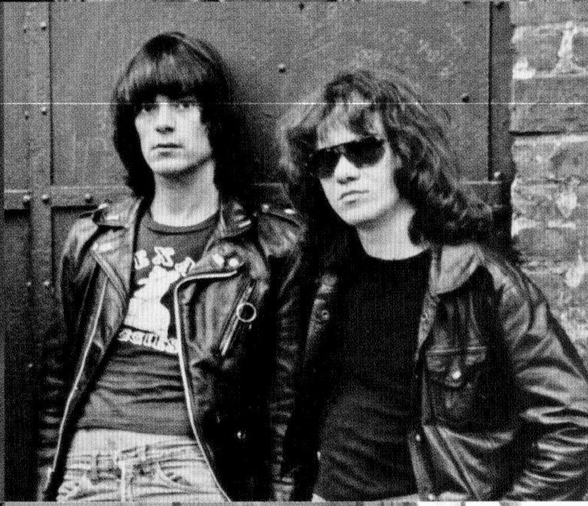
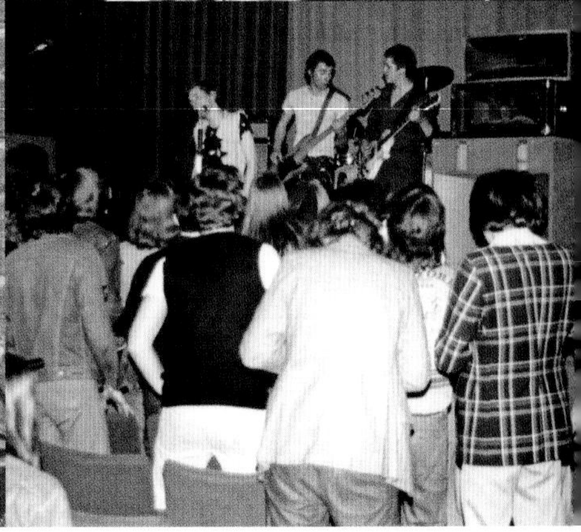
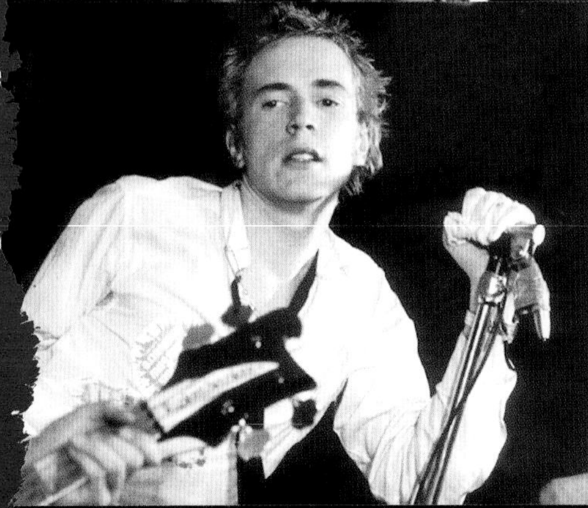
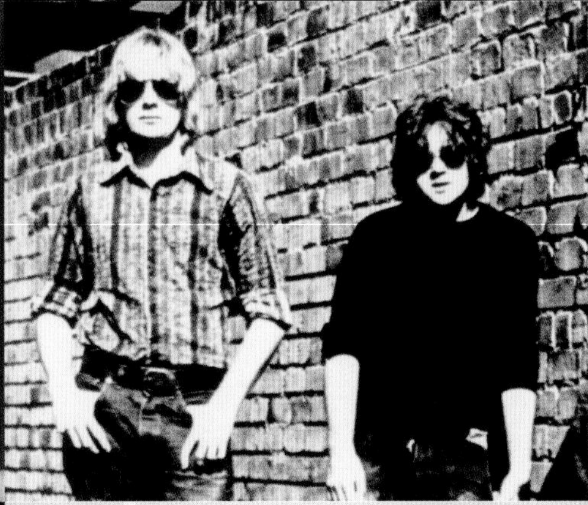
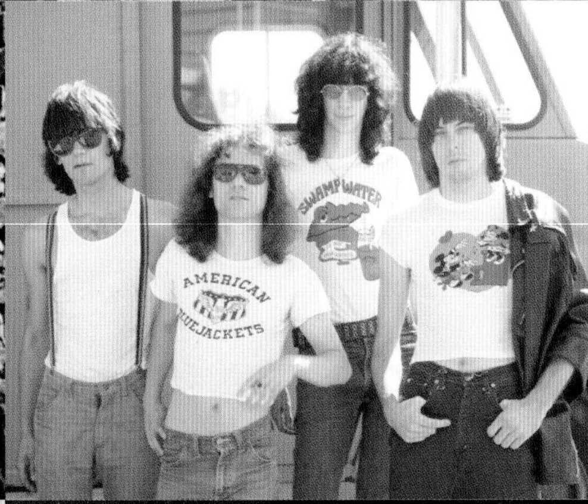

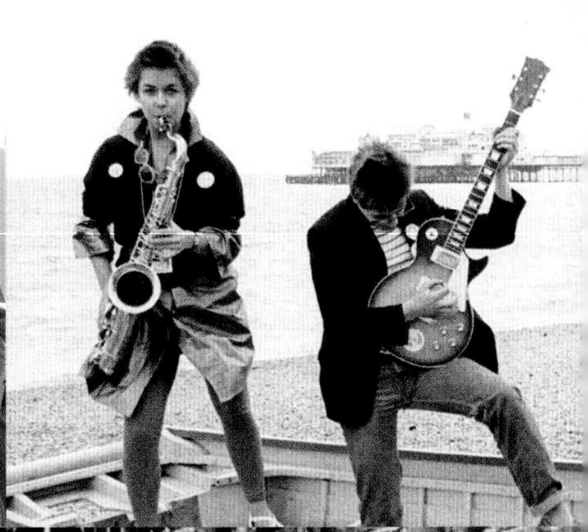
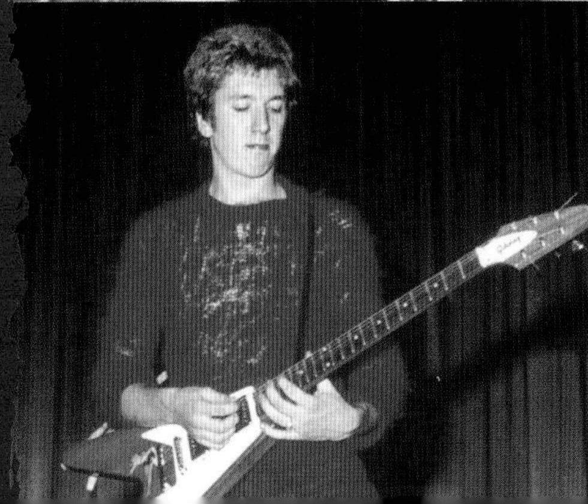
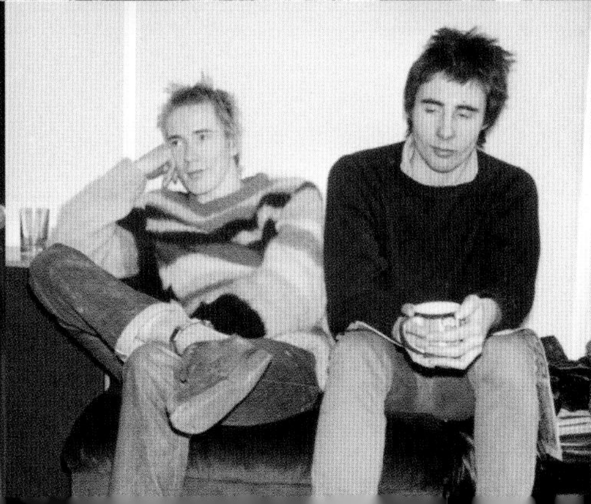
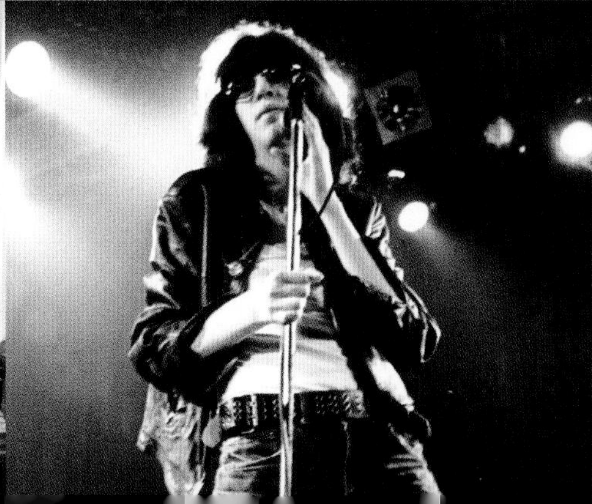
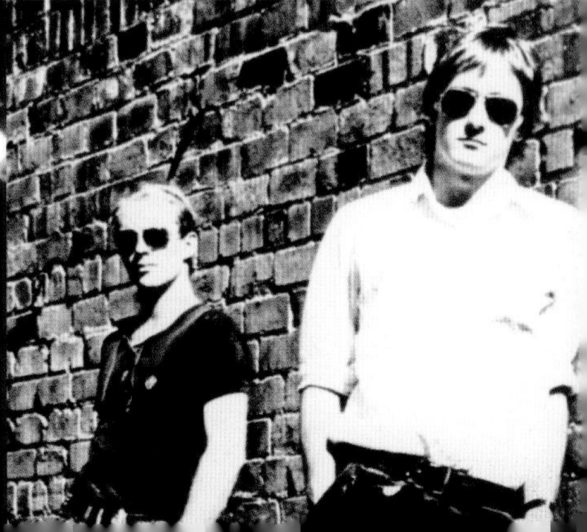

1976

By early 1976, The Sex Pistols were playing intermittent gigs in London, getting a reputation for the random acts of violence that surrounded their shows. They were also inspiring others to form punk bands – notably London SS, who never released a record or even played a note in public but were directly responsible for the formation of The Clash and Generation X, and indirectly responsible for many more.

In New York, The Ramones raised the flag with their 'Blitzkrieg Bop' single and debut album. In London they fanned the flames of the emerging punk scene, and then did the same in Los Angeles and Toronto. Australia needed no such help; bands like The Saints were already primed and waiting to go. In the wake of The Ramones, the New York scene bubbled with new bands and lured the notorious Dead Boys from Cleveland.

In London the scene still centred around The Sex Pistols, whose gigs provided a platform for emerging bands like The Clash, Buzzcocks, The Vibrators and The Damned, who were first to get a record out. But it was The Sex Pistols' snarling 'Anarchy In The UK' that got the media frothing, while the band's undeleted expletives on TV caused a frenzy.

St. MARTINS SCHOOL
FIRST GIG
Sex Pistols
November 6th 1975
'UNPLUGGED'
OF ART

1976

EARLY

THE SEX PISTOLS' FIRST GIGS

The Sex Pistols played their first gig at London's St Martin's School of Art in November 1975, racing through a batch of Faces and Who numbers plus some of their own, including 'Pretty Vacant' and 'Did You No Wrong', while Rotten sneered at the audience, calling them 'f***ing boring'. The pattern was repeated at isolated shows around London in early 1976 but promoters were reluctant to book them because an aura of violence hung over their shows. There were instances of journalists and punters being beaten up and Rotten even tried to goad Glen Matlock into a fight on stage at the 100 Club, storming off stage when he couldn't.

EARLY

LONDON STORMTROOPERS

As The Sex Pistols' antics raised punk's profile, several bands sprang up around London looking for a way to join in. The provocatively named London SS was formed in March 1975 by guitarist Mick Jones and bassist Tony James (pictured opposite). They never actually played a gig or released a record but, over a period of nine months, what would become a Who's Who of the punk scene auditioned for the line-up, including Brian James and Chris Miller (a.k.a. Rat Scabies), who would shortly form The Damned, Chrissie Hynde (The Pretenders) and Matt Dangerfield (The Boys). When the band ran out of people to audition, James switched to guitar and joined Chelsea before forming Generation X.

EARLY

RICHARD HELL FALLS INTO THE VOIDOIDS

Richard Hell lasted nine months in The Heartbreakers before quitting early in 1976, describing them as 'too brutish'. After failing to settle in two bands, the obvious solution was to start his own. Hell duly formed The Voidoids to back him on songs he'd had since his days in Television, including the seminal punk anthem 'Blank Generation' with its opening lyrics, 'I was saying "Let me out of here" before I was even born'. Malcolm McLaren had tried unsuccessfully to get Hell to relocate to London, believing that he had the 'perfect punk image'.

APRIL

THE COMING OF THE CLASH

After London SS imploded at the start of 1976, Mick Jones took up with drummer Terry Chimes and one-time vocalist Paul Simonon, now on bass. Malcolm McLaren's assistant Bernie Rhodes, who had tried and failed to bring some order to London SS, stayed with Jones and together they looked for a singer. In April 1976, after a gig by The 101'ers at London's Nashville Rooms (where they were supported by The Sex Pistols), Rhodes and Jones approached lead singer/guitarist John Mellor, who had recently renamed himself Joe Strummer. Simonon gave the new band their name – The Clash – and they played their first gig, supporting The Sex Pistols, in Sheffield in July 1976.

APRIL

THE RAMONES' 'BLITZKRIEG BOP'

The definitive sound of punk finally made it onto record in April 1976 when The Ramones' first single, 'Blitzkrieg Bop', was released. Relentlessly pummelling the same three chords for two minutes and 12 seconds, the band captured the raucous audience excitement of their shows, right from the opening chant of 'Hey! Ho! Let's Go!'. Although it's regarded as an undisputed punk anthem, Joey Ramone admitted that the idea of the song actually came from listening to British teenypop band The Bay City Rollers' hit 'Saturday Night'. 'It had a great chant in it, so we wanted a song with a chant in it.'

APRIL

THE RAMONES' FIRST ALBUM

Recorded for a paltry $6,400 that probably wouldn't have covered the cost of an Eagles backing track, The Ramones' self-titled first album distilled punk rock down to its bare essentials. Less concerned with hi-fi than with making an impact, the 14 two-minute songs clattered by with a deceptive production-line monotony, enhanced by Joey Ramone's barely decipherable lyrics and the band's dense, minimalist sound. The result was a succession of instant anthems: 'Blitzkrieg Bop', 'Beat On The Brat', 'Judy Is A Punk', 'I Wanna Be Your Boyfriend' and 'Now I Wanna Sniff Some Glue'. They even displayed a trace of irony, printing the lyrics on the inner sleeve.

JUNE

THE SEX PISTOLS TAKE MANCHESTER

On 4 June 1976, The Sex Pistols played at Manchester's Lesser Free Trade Hall, a gig that has been credited with launching the punk movement there and consequently starting some of the city's most famous bands. The venue had a capacity of 150 but more than 10 times that number now claim to have been there. In fact it's estimated that around 40 people turned up. But among those definitely in that select crowd were Morrissey, who would go on to form The Smiths, members of Buzzcocks, Mark E Smith (The Fall) and Bernard Sumner and Peter Hook (Joy Division and later New Order).

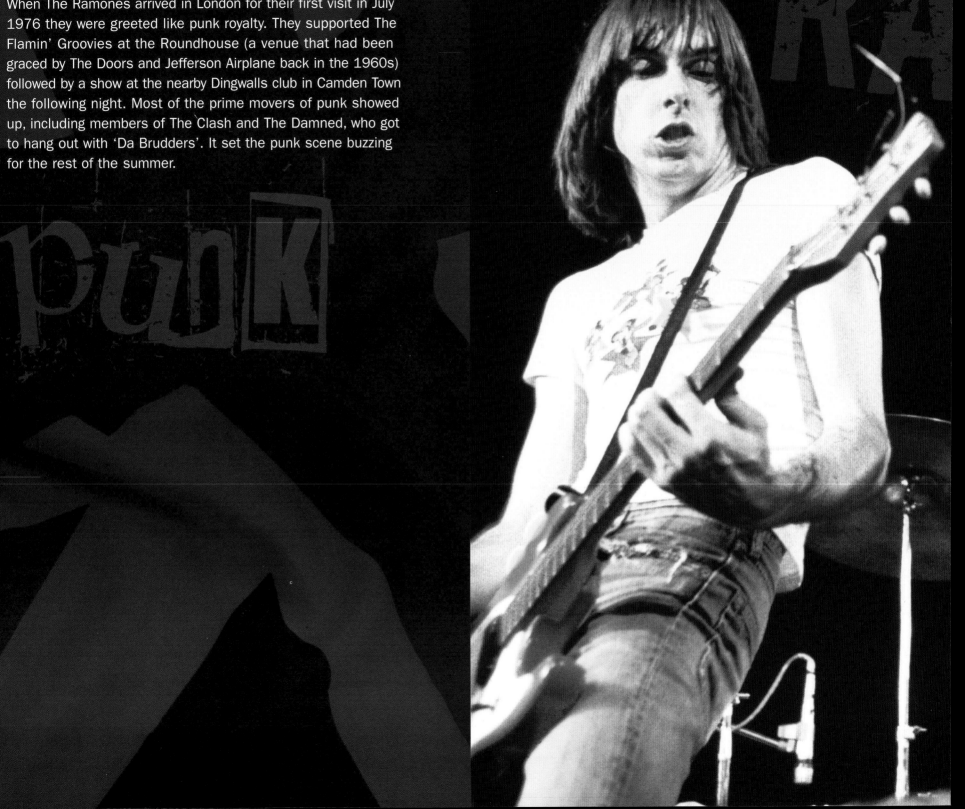

When The Ramones arrived in London for their first visit in July 1976 they were greeted like punk royalty. They supported The Flamin' Groovies at the Roundhouse (a venue that had been graced by The Doors and Jefferson Airplane back in the 1960s) followed by a show at the nearby Dingwalls club in Camden Town the following night. Most of the prime movers of punk showed up, including members of The Clash and The Damned, who got to hang out with 'Da Brudders'. It set the punk scene buzzing for the rest of the summer.

July

BUZZCOCKS AT THE READY

The Sex Pistols returned to Manchester in July 1976 and were supported by local band Buzzcocks. Bolton art students Howard Devoto and Pete Shelley had travelled to see The Sex Pistols play in High Wycombe in February, and were inspired not just to form their own band but also to set up The Pistols' first Manchester gig in June. They had intended to play that gig but they had problems finding a like-minded bassist and drummer. At the gig Malcolm McLaren introduced them to one of the audience, Steve Diggle, who would join them on bass. Buzzcocks were soon ready.

July

THE DEAD BOYS ALIVE AND KICKING

Punk didn't get more extreme than The Dead Boys, who came charging out of Cleveland in the middle of 1976 and took the hardened New York scene by storm. Fronted by singer Stiv Bators, the band were originally known as Frankenstein. But punk outlets were hard to find in Cleveland and when Joey Ramone urged them to move to New York they jumped at the chance, changing their name to The Dead Boys. Their shows were notorious for violence and vulgar behaviour, with Bators frequently attempting to mutilate himself with the mike stand. Their motto was 'F*** Art, Let's Dance', encapsulated on their furious classic punk anthem 'Sonic Reducer'.

THE RAMONES AT THE ROXY LA

After their successful show in London, The Ramones and The Flamin' Groovies joined forces again for a gig at the Roxy in Los Angeles on 11 August 1976. The gig is generally credited with kick-starting the LA punk scene. Punk was not an easy sell in sun-kissed California but what the audience lacked in numbers they made up for with enthusiasm, as The Ramones delivered their now well-honed 16-song set. And the Roxy cashed in by becoming the leading punk venue in the city for the next decade. In all, The Ramones played a dozen dates in California that month.

AUGUST

MIDNIGHT SPECIAL ON THE GREEN

The burgeoning British punk movement got its first chance to show off at the end of August 1976, when The Sex Pistols headlined a Midnight Special at London's Screen On The Green cinema in Islington. They were supported by The Clash (pictured opposite) playing only their third gig and Buzzcocks, who were making their first London appearance. The show was something of a media event, with the photographers paying almost as much attention to the fans as the bands. The self-styled Bromley Contingent, who were at the forefront of the punk fashion scene, were out in force, their number including Siouxsie Sioux, Steve Severin, Billy Idol, Jordan and Soo Catwoman.

SEPTEMBER

THE RAMONES IN TORONTO

Having galvanized the punk scene in New York, London and Los Angeles, The Ramones continued their ambassadorial role by bringing punk to Canada in September. They played two nights at Toronto's New Yorker Theatre, a cinema that had a stage specially installed. They started with their trademark opening with Joey Ramone staring at the audience as the feedback built up behind him saying, 'Good evening. We're The Ramones. You're a loudmouth baby, you better shut it up,' before the inevitable '1-2-3-4!' The only criticism appears to have been that they were wearing new jeans.

SEPTEMBER

THE CANADIAN SCENE

The Ramones' Toronto show sparked the formation of several local bands, the most infamous of which were The Viletones fronted by Steven Leckie (a.k.a. Nazi Dog). Their first show produced headlines of the 'Not them, not here' variety. The frantic power-pop of The Diodes was more readily acceptable but punk had a hard time breaking through. The city's first punk club, Crash 'n' Burn, lasted just four months, but fans (like those pictured right) were quick to adpot punk's look and attitude. Further west, The Furies were Vancouver's first punk band followed by The Modernettes and The Pointed Sticks. But Canada's geography made touring tough. However, the country can claim the first three all-girl punk bands: The Curse, The B-Girls and The Dishrags.

PUNK DOWN UNDER

Australia's punk roots go back to 1973 when singer Chris Bailey and guitarist Ed Kuepper founded The Saints in Brisbane. They found it hard to get gigs so they set up in a house. They were inevitably busted by the police, which only stirred up more interest, and by 1974 there was an active punk scene in the city. It spread to Sydney where Radio Birdman were formed by Detroit immigrant Deniz Tek. In Melbourne a young Nick Cave co-founded Boys Next Door. But it was The Saints (pictured opposite) who got a single out first – '(I'm) Stranded' in September 1976. A copy arrived at British music magazine *Sounds*, who promptly declared it Single Of The Week. Within weeks they were signed to EMI Records.

THE SEX PISTOLS ON THE ROAD

Immediately after their Screen On The Green show, The Sex Pistols travelled to Paris to open the Club de Chalet. The Bromley Contingent tagged along to add a bit of punk chic. From there the band flew to Manchester to make their TV debut on the Granada TV show *So It Goes*, compered by Tony Wilson. As the band cranked up the opening of 'Anarchy In The UK' Johnny Rotten sneered 'Get off your arse'. For the next couple of months The Sex Pistols played low-key dates around Britain, including one at Chelmsford Prison. It was the most sustained bout of touring they would ever do.

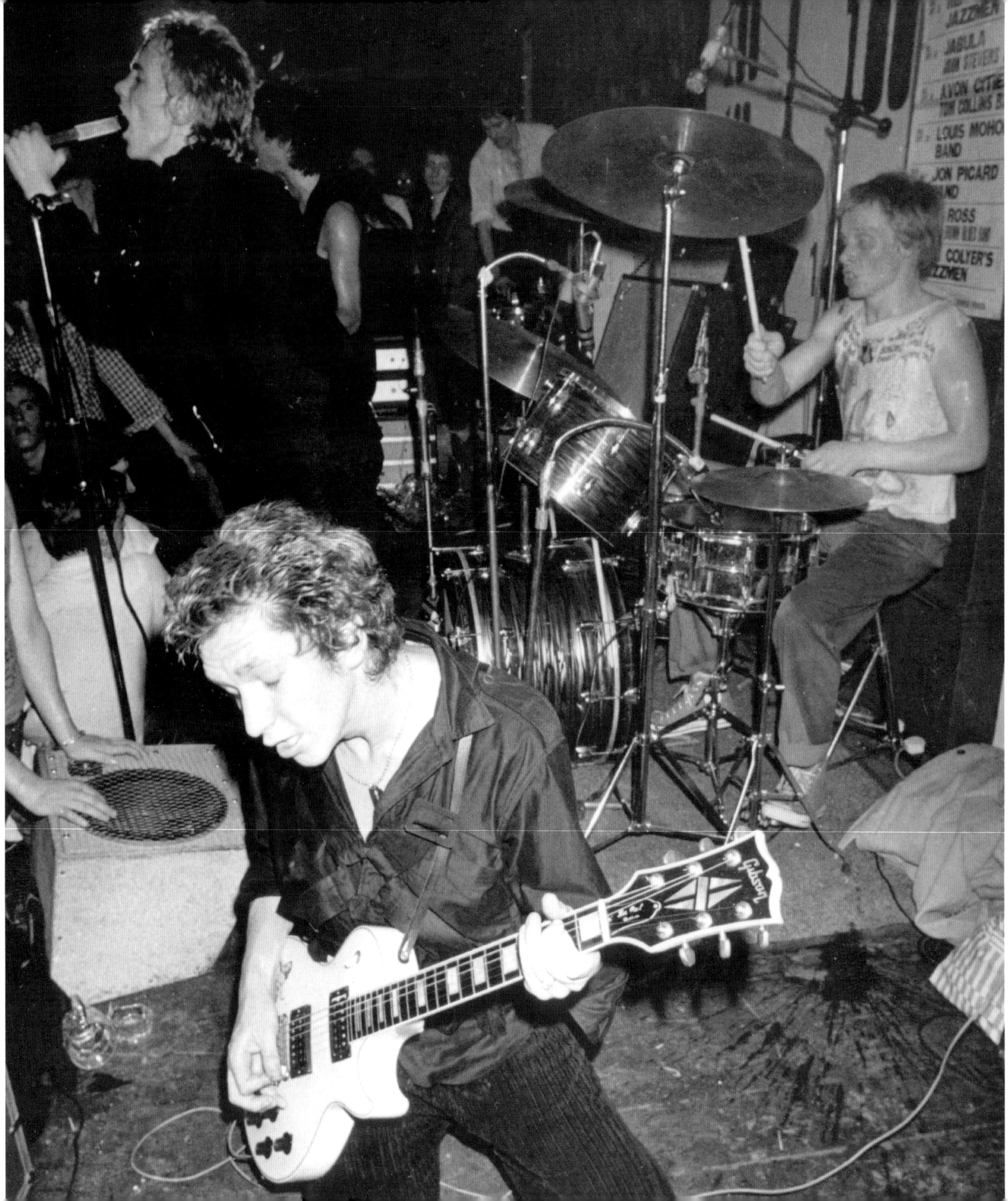
JAZZMEN
JABULA
JON PICARD
BAND
Gibson

SEPTEMBER

100 CLUB PUNK SPECIAL

Piqued at being barred from appearing at the first punk rock festival at Mont de Marson in southern France during the summer of 1976 because of the violence surrounding Sex Pistols gigs, Malcolm McLaren staged his own two-day punk festival at London's 100 Club on September 20 and 21. The Sex Pistols (pictured opposite) headlined the first night with The Clash, while Siouxsie & The Banshees and Subway Sect played their first shows. Buzzcocks headlined the second night with The Damned, The Vibrators and French punk band Stinky Toys. The second night was marred when a glass was thrown (allegedly by Sid Vicious), wounding a girl in the eye. Punk gigs were promptly banned by the 100 Club.

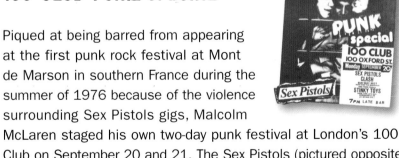

SEPTEMBER

SIOUXSIE GOES FROM BROMLEY TO BANSHEE

Siouxsie Sioux of the Bromley Contingent wore a provocative outfit of fetish clothing with swastika arm bands that was guaranteed to offend if everything else failed. Following the punk ethic that 'Anyone could do it', she put a band together with her boyfriend Steve Severin during the summer of 1976. Three days before the 100 Club Punk Special, she suggested to Malcolm McLaren that they could fill in for a band that had dropped out. When Malcolm agreed they hurriedly roped in some mates from the Sex boutique crowd: Marco Pirroni on guitar and Sid Vicious on drums. Their set consisted of a 20-minute freestyle piece called 'The Lord's Prayer' that incorporated bits of 'Twist And Shout' and 'Smoke On The Water'.

NEW BANDS EMERGE

The buzz that was building around the punk scene in
the autumn of 1976 resulted in an upsurge of new bands.
Tony James, who'd tried to form London SS with Mick Jones,
joined Chelsea, fronted by Gene October, where he played with
guitarist Billy Idol and drummer John Towe. A couple of months
later, the three of them left October to form Generation X, and
were the first band to play the new London punk club, the Roxy,
in December 1976. The Stranglers (pictured left) meanwhile
were no spring chickens when punk arrived, having formed in
1974 with blues, classical and jazz influences. But successful
support slots with Patti Smith and The Ramones on their first
British gigs gave them a free pass.

AUTUMN

MORE NEW BANDS APPEAR

Subway Sect were a bunch of South London soul boys who'd
started hanging out at Sex Pistols gigs and were encouraged
to become a band by Malcolm McLaren. The Nipple Erectors,
formed by punk artist Shanne Bradley, featured a youthful
Shane McGowan, then known as Shane O'Hooligan. Eater were
North London schoolkids playing speeded-up versions of Velvet
Underground classics. X-Ray Spex (pictured opposite) featured
the piercing vocals, thick teeth braces and costumes from the
dressing-up box of Poly Styrene and her memorable anthem,
'Oh Bondage, Up Yours!'. Arriving in London from rural Devon,
punk couple TV Smith and Gaye Advert formed The Adverts,
who had another ready-made punk anthem, 'Bored Teenagers'.

OCTOBER

THE SEX PISTOLS SIGN TO EMI

In October 1976 The Sex Pistols signed to EMI Records, the biggest British record label and home to The Beatles, Queen and Pink Floyd. The band had been expected to make a deal with one of the leading independent labels and signing with such a prestigious company surprised many in the punk movement, not to mention EMI Records themselves. The band's £40,000 advance was not an excessive risk for EMI. The band were promptly dispatched to the studio with their own engineer, Dave Goodman. The results were rejected by EMI's A&R department and the band sent back to the studio with house producer Chris Thomas, who had worked with The Beatles, Pink Floyd and Roxy Music.

PATTI SMITH TUNES INTO RADIO ETHIOPIA

Patti Smith's second album, RADIO ETHIOPIA, divided the critics when it was released in October 1976. Smith had chosen producer Jack Douglas to make a more commercially appealing record but critics accused her of selling out. The sprawling, 10-minute title track in particular polarized opinions, being either 'visionary' or 'self-indulgent'. There were complaints that the heavy whining guitars drowned out Smith's voice, although some argued that on 'Pissing In The River' this was a blessing, as the lyrics fell short of the standard she'd set on 'Piss Factory'.

It was telling that the album was credited to the Patti Smith Group rather than simply Smith as it had been on HORSES.

THE DAMNED'S 'NEW ROSE'

The Damned claimed the honour of releasing the first British punk single in October 1976. They featured singer Dave Vanian, who combined business as a gravedigger with pleasure as a Goth, guitarist Brian James and drummer Rat Scabies, who both had London SS connections, and Scabies' mate, genial nutter Captain Sensible on bass. They formed in May 1976, played their first gig supporting The Sex Pistols at London's 100 Club in July, and signed to independent label Stiff Records a month later. 'New Rose' was a frantic tale of teen angst referenced by a quote from The Shangri-La's 'Leader Of The Pack' – 'Is she really going out with him?' – at the start. The B-side was a cover of The Beatles' 'Help' taken at twice the speed of the original.

NOVEMBER

THE VIBRATORS VIBRATE

A year earlier the Vibrators had been one of the new breed of energetic R&B bands. But they'd embraced punk with gusto and were an obvious choice to play the 100 Club's Punk Special, where they were joined on stage by respected rock session guitarist Chris Spedding. He introduced them to producer Mickie Most, whose hit career stretched from Suzi Quatro and Hot Chocolate back to Jeff Beck and The Animals. He produced their first single, 'We Vibrate', which was released in November 1976. It still contained R&B influences and sounded too clean to satisfy the die-hard punks, but it came out ahead of The Sex Pistols' debut single released later that month.

NOVEMBER

THE CRAMPS GO PUNK

The Cramps had been formed in 1973 in California by the delightfully named Lux Interior and his equally delightfully named wife Poison Ivy. The band combined their fascination with horror movie schlock, rockabilly and surf music. They built up a small cult following before moving to New York in 1975, where their raw, grungy sound and Interior's macabre, sexually charged on-stage persona was a natural fit with the emerging punk movement. They made their debut at CBGBs, supporting The Dead Boys in November 1976, and quickly became a regular fixture there as well as at Max's Kansas City.

NOVEMBER

ANARCHY REIGNS FOR THE PISTOLS

With Johnny Rotten's cackled 'Right... Now' rising above Steve Jones' blistering, metronomic guitar riff, The Sex Pistols finally unleashed their first single on 26 November 1976. 'Anarchy In The UK' reflected all the pent-up frustration, energy and anticipation of recent months. While the band blasted out their big, defiant sound, Rotten revelled in his deliberately provocative lyrics, stirring the pot with a snarl and daring you to get the joke with a sneer. The single made modest progress up the charts in the run-up to Christmas – not, it must be said, the prime season for anarchy and rebellion – and finally cracked the UK Top 40 at the end of the year.

DECEMBER

PISTOLS' FILTH AND MEDIA FURY

On 1 December, less than a week after the release of 'Anarchy In The UK', The Sex Pistols appeared on the Thames TV early evening magazine programme *Today*, broadcast across the London area. The inebriated and unsympathetic presenter faced a sullen and bored group, while members of the Bromley Contingent standing behind the band goaded both sides on. When Grundy misunderstood a comment from Siouxsie Sioux and made an inappropriate remark, Steve Jones called him 'a dirty sod', 'a dirty old man', 'a dirty b***ard' and finally, after being urged to continue by Grundy, 'a dirty f***er'. Cue credits, cue hysterical media outrage.

DECEMBER

ANARCHY DERAILED FOR THE PISTOLS

Amid the furore that followed The Sex Pistols' *Today* appearance – which cost Bill Grundy his job – the planned UK tour with The Damned, The Clash and The Heartbreakers to promote the single was almost totally derailed. Sixteen of the 19 scheduled dates were cancelled by local authorities, frequently at short notice. In Derby, the town councillors demanded that the band perform an audition before they were allowed to play. The band declined. Even worse, Paul Cook's mum told *The Daily Mail* that he was no longer welcome at home and his bedroom was being turned into a dining room.

THE SECOND WAVE: 1977–78

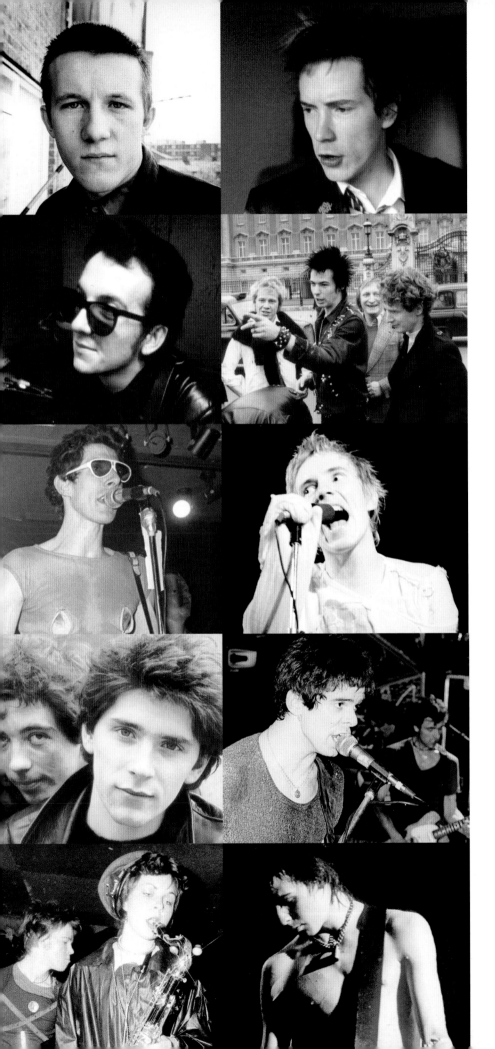

1977-78

As The Sex Pistols passed through three record companies in the first half of 1977, sacked their song-writing bass player for liking The Beatles and struggled to find venues that would let them play, they became a side-show in the thriving British punk scene now led by The Clash.

In London, new punk clubs sprang up and found no shortage of bands to book: Generation X, X-Ray Spex, The Adverts, Subway Sect and Wire. In New York the diversity of bands on display meant that there was something for almost every taste, from the cerebral Television and Talking Heads to The Dead Boys' outrageousness, with Richard Hell somewhere in between. Meanwhile, The Ramones refined their garage/surf/punk style to the point of commercialism. The West Coast scene was hotting up in Los Angeles with The Weirdos and The Germs, and in San Francisco with The Nuns and The Mutants.

Early in 1978 The Sex Pistols, who six months earlier had set the British establishment aquiver as they mocked the Queen's Silver Jubilee, disintegrated into farce after an American tour. But British punk had found its voice, as was forcefully shown at a Rock Against Racism concert in London's Victoria Park, headlined by The Clash, that attracted some 80,000 people.

1977

JANUARY

THE SEX PISTOLS GET THE BULLET

On 6 January 1977 EMI Records terminated its contract with The Sex Pistols, saying it was unable to promote the group's records 'in view of the adverse publicity generated over the past two months'. The media furore over the Pistols' TV appearance six weeks earlier had barely abated and now politicians were weighing in as the nation's moral guardians. Conservative MP for Christchurch and Lymington, Robert Adley, had written to EMI managing director Sir John Reed suggesting that a company of EMI's reputation should 'forgo the doubtful privilege of sponsoring trash like The Sex Pistols'. However, the band got to keep their £40,000 advance.

JANUARY

SECOND SERVING FOR THE RAMONES

Just eight months after their first album, during which time they'd spread the word across North America and the UK, The Ramones unveiled more of the same on LEAVE HOME. Once again they rattled through 14 songs in less than half an hour, although the success of the first album meant they got a bigger production budget. It allowed the band to refine their sound and smooth out a few rough edges, but otherwise the format stayed much the same, with songs about freaks ('Pinhead'), misogyny ('Glad To See You Go') and substance abuse ('Carbona Not Glue'). In fact the last track was withdrawn in America after complaints.

JANUARY

THE CLASH SIGN UP

While The Sex Pistols were generating all the headlines, it was The Clash that the record companies were really interested in signing. Although they'd played fewer than 30 gigs by the beginning of 1977, they were more focussed and more rehearsed, and in late January they signed to CBS after a bidding war with Polydor Records, who had also battled with EMI to sign The Pistols. They received an advance of £100,000, an unprecedented amount at the time, but they had to pay all their recording and artwork expenses from this sum and there were other clauses in the contract that would later cost them dear.

JANUARY

FANZINES KEEP THE FAITH

Needless to say, The Clash were accused of selling out by many in the punk scene. The editor of UK fanzine *Sniffin' Glue*, Mark P (pictured opposite), declared that 'Punk died the day The Clash signed to CBS'. Bank clerk Mark P had started *Sniffin' Glue* as a Xeroxed fanzine, selling 50 copies of the first issue. That soon grew to around 15,000 copies but Mark never deviated from his DIY punk ethic. Another fanzine, *Sideburns*, produced one of punk's great iconic images in its January 1977 issue with an illustration of three guitar chord shapes captioned, 'This is a chord, this is another chord, this is a third. Now form a band.'

JANUARY

BUZZCOCKS SCRATCH THE ITCH

At least Buzzcocks stayed true to punk's DIY ethic. Borrowing £500 from families and friends, they recorded and pressed up 1,000 copies of an EP called **SPIRAL SCRATCH**. Produced by Martin Hannett (who would become a leading producer over the next decade) and recorded in one three-hour session, the four-track EP featured the minimalist punk gem, 'Boredom'. Released on their own New Hormones label at the end of January 1977, the initial pressing quickly sold out and they went on to sell another 15,000 through mail order and the Manchester Virgin record store.

JANUARY

THE ROXY, WC2

London got its first dedicated punk venue at the beginning of 1977, when the Roxy opened up in Covent Garden in a cellar beneath a small bar. There was no shortage of new and up-and-coming bands looking for a gig and the club quickly became a mecca for punk wannabes jumping – or pogo-ing – aboard the bandwagon. The club's first 100 days were documented on the live album, **THE ROXY LONDON WC2**, featuring low-fi versions of punk classics 'Oh Bondage, Up Yours!' by X-Ray Spex (pictured opposite), 'Bored Teenagers' by The Adverts and '1 2 X U' by Wire. The tracks were segued by eavesdropped conversations in the bar and toilets.

TELEVISION SHOOT FOR THE MOON

With the punk ethic exerting a stronger grip at the start of 1977, the punk aesthetic also got a major boost with the release of Television's eagerly awaited debut album, MARQUEE MOON, on 8 February. After Richard Hell's departure, Tom Verlaine had refashioned the band around his tense, brittle interplay with fellow guitarist Richard Lloyd. MARQUEE MOON harnessed their new brand of guitar rock with a punk sensibility and literate lyrics. They weren't afraid to expand the punk template either: the absorbing title track that finally releases the tension that's been building inside their musical pressure cooker runs for a most un-punk-like 10 minutes. This was followed by the less well-received ADVENTURE in April 1978. The band split later that year, with Lloyd and Verlaine intent on pursuing solo careers.

DAMNED DAMNED DAMNED

First with a punk single, now first with an album, The Damned's triple self-titled debut album was released by Stiff Records on 18 February 1977. With a dozen tracks lasting less than half an hour and a suitably ragged production by Nick Lowe (pictured above in the dustbin), the album embellished the fast and furious template laid down by their 'New Rose' single, from the full-on thrash of 'Neat Neat Neat' to the brief staccato jerk of drummer Rat Scabies' 'Stab Yor Back'. The album even made a brief appearance in the UK Top 40. In a frankly unfathomable promotional gambit, Stiff deliberately put a picture of Eddie & The Hot Rods on the back cover instead of The Damned and then printed an erratum slip.

FEBRUARY

SID COCKS HIS PISTOL

With The Sex Pistols on hiatus, the growing ill-feeling towards bassist Glen Matlock by the rest of the band came to a head and he left in February 1977. The official explanation was that he 'liked The Beatles', although Matlock later said he was 'sick of all the bull$h!t'. Matlock co-wrote 10 of the 12 tracks on the band's debut album, **NEVER MIND THE BOLLOCKS**..., which wasn't released until October. He was replaced by Sid Vicious, who was better known for random acts of violence than bass playing. In fact, he had never played bass before. It was while he was learning and trying to rehearse with the band that he met American teenage delinquent Nancy Spungen (pictured in the background) who was hanging around the fringes of the UK punk scene.

MARCH

THE SEX PISTOLS SIGN TO A&M

At a staged event outside Buckingham Palace on 10 March 1977, The Sex Pistols signed a new record deal with A&M Records and announced that their next single would celebrate the Queen's Silver Jubilee. At a party at A&M's offices afterwards, members of the group abused record company staff. Sid Vicious trailed blood around the offices from a cut foot, sustained in breaking a toilet bowl. Six days later, after Sid Vicious was involved in a fight at the Speakeasy Club with TV/radio presenter Bob Harris and an engineer who required 14 stitches to a head wound, A&M terminated the contract.

THE DAMNED TEAM UP WITH T. REX

To promote their new single, 'Neat Neat Neat', and their **DAMNED DAMNED DAMNED** album, The Damned (pictured above) headed out on a UK tour in March supporting T. Rex. It was an unusual pairing that raised eyebrows in the media, not least because Marc Bolan was rebuilding a career that had come to a juddering halt a couple of years earlier. But the tour was beneficial to both acts. Damned fans got to see a glam legend back on form, while T. Rex fans got their first punk experience. Or as Marc Bolan put it, 'We'll see who can out-punk the other every night.'

THE CLASH WANNA RIOT

The Clash, who'd been having drummer problems since signing to CBS, with founder drummer Terry Chimes leaving and then returning to record with them before leaving again, released their first single, 'White Riot', in March. Frantic, powerful and overtly political, it was written by Joe Strummer after he'd been caught up in the Notting Hill riots between black youths and the police the previous summer. According to Paul Simonon, the song was about 'white people getting up and doing it for themselves'. After peaking at No. 38 in the UK charts, the single spent over seven months knocking around the lower regions of the chart.

APRIL

THE DAMNED TOUR THE US

The Damned continued their pioneering ways with their first American tour in April 1977. They started with four nights at CBGBs in New York supporting The Dead Boys before moving on for two nights at Boston's Rat Club. Then they flew to the West Coast, where they played Los Angeles shows at the Whisky a Go Go and the Starwood, finishing up with two nights at the San Francisco Mabuhay Gardens. While they were well received everywhere, there was the occasional cultural mishap. Dave Vanian remembered, 'One club we played everyone was sitting in front of us eating pizza. We were so outraged that we pulled up a table on stage, got a tablecloth, ordered a pizza and ate it while they were watching. Then they got outraged.'

APRIL

WEST COAST PUNKS

The Damned's California shows on their US tour acted as a focal point for the emerging West Coast punk scene. Captain Sensible jammed with Los Angeles punk-art rockers The Weirdos. The support band was The Germs, playing their first gig and, according to guitarist Pat Smear, 'We had no songs or anything.... We made a noise for five minutes until they threw us off.' New bands at that time ranged from risqué surrealists Black Randy & The Metrosquad and the more literate X (pictured above) to the Chicano punk of The Plugz. In the San Francisco Bay area, pioneering punks The Nuns were building a crowd. Theatrical punks The Mutants were another popular attraction. Meanwhile, bored folk singer Penelope Houston was about to go from a whisper to a scream with The Avengers.

THE CLASH'S CAREER OPPORTUNITY

While The Sex Pistols fiddled, The Clash burned. They didn't spend long recording their self-titled first album, released in April 1977. They had something to say and, rather than trying to cover up their musical inexperience, they simply muddied the sound. The result was an onslaught of venom and sardonic humour enmeshed in flaming guitars and raw rhythms. The lyrics were hard to hear but there if you listened: rants against the welfare state ('Career Opportunities'), drug addiction ('Deny'), the so-called working class ('48 Hours') and imperialism ('I'm So Bored With The USA'). **THE CLASH** was a visceral thrill. In the UK the album was a breakthrough, reaching No. 12. In the US, CBS chose not to release the album and then watched as it sold 100,000 on import.

THE STRANGLERS GET A GRIP

The Stranglers may have been derided by die-hard punks for their pub-rock roots and sexist sleaze, but the wider public had no such qualms. They'd supported The Ramones and Patti Smith; their credentials were good. And their keyboard-driven sound marked them out amid the cacophony of thrashing guitars. Plus they had some great tunes: 'Peaches' and 'Something Better Change' were both UK Top 10 hits over the summer of 1977 and their **RATTUS NORVEGICUS** debut album released in April 1977 made No. 4 in the UK charts. Just to prove it was no fluke, they did it again later in the year with **NO MORE HEROES**, which got to No. 2.

APRIL

THE JAM ADD MOD CONS

Formed in the London commuter town of Woking, The Jam combined the high energy of punk with a sharp mod-revival image. The trio, led by singer/guitarist Paul Weller, stood out from the punk scene when they started playing London gigs in 1976, with their mohair suits and slick performances. But the songs, influenced by early Who and Small Faces and condensed into brief, staccato hooks and angry, articulate lyrics, were a perfect match for punk and the band supported The Sex Pistols on several gigs. They signed to Polydor Records in 1977 and their first single, 'In The City', released in April, confirmed their mastery of punk-pop, becoming a Top 40 hit.

MAY

THE POLICE FALL OUT

A trio formed by former Curved Air drummer Stewart Copeland and Newcastle-born bassist Sting, who had recently moved down to London, together with French guitarist Henry Padovani, The Police released their first single on their own independent label, Illegal Records, called 'Fall Out' on 1 May 1977. It certainly sounded punk and the band were picking up support slots at punk gigs around London, but the media were suspicious of Copeland's prog-rock background and Sting's jazz-rock affiliations. In fact only Padovani (pictured right) appeared to have the correct credentials.

THE CLASH

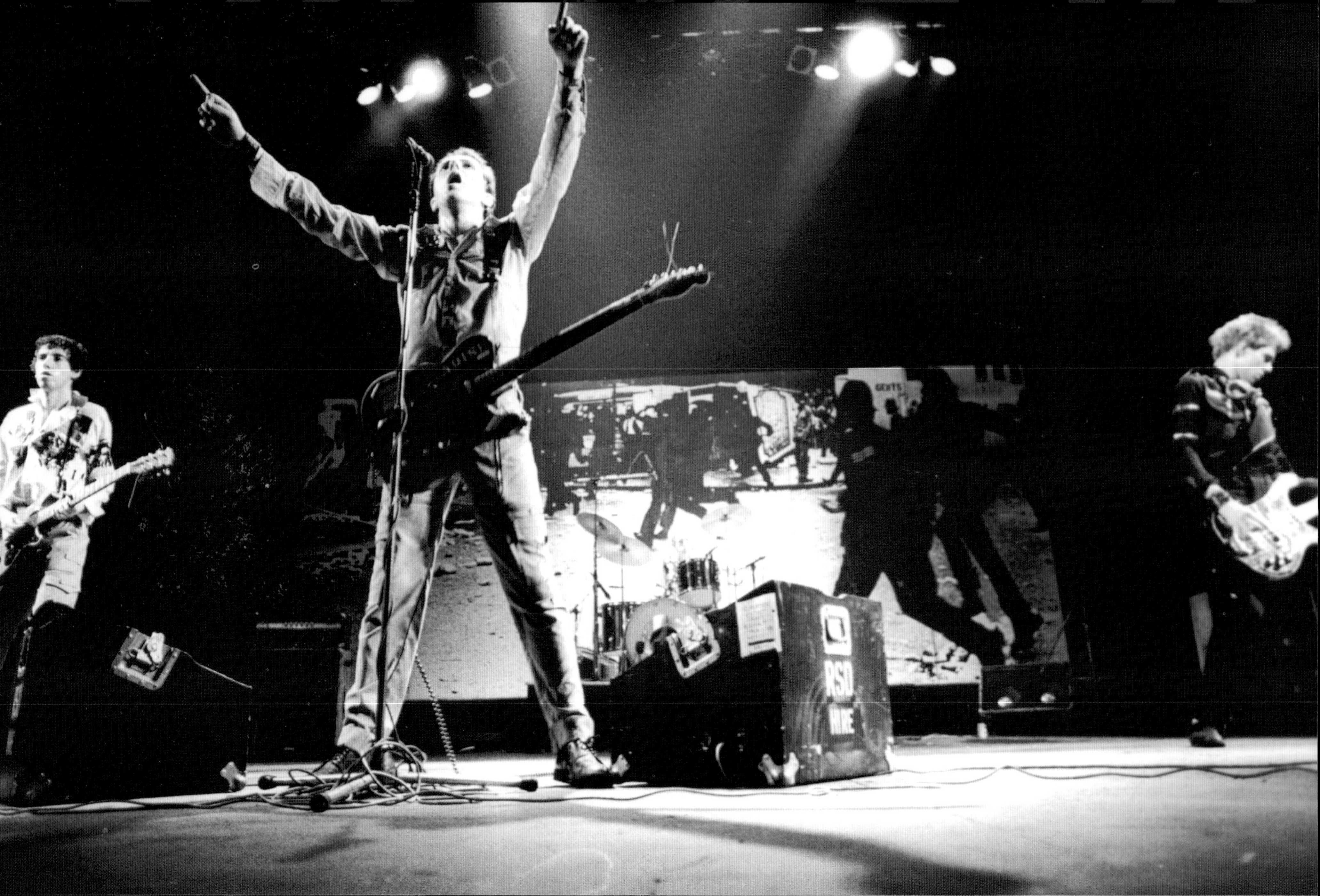

THE CLASH

MAY

THE CLASH ON TOUR

At the beginning of May, The Clash headed out on their White Riot tour of Britain – 25 dates in 30 days. It was the first time that a full punk show had been staged in cities like Newcastle and Edinburgh, and the media attention was intense as punk was still viewed as a serious threat to the nation's moral fibre. However, apart from a few rows of seats being trashed at London's Rainbow Theatre, there was little damage at the gigs. But the media were able to gleefully report that Joe Strummer and Mick Jones were arrested and detained overnight in Newcastle for the alleged theft of a pillowcase. That's right, a pillowcase.

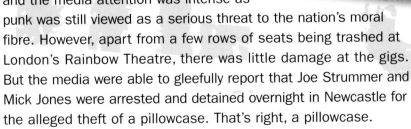

SWANSEA UNIVERSITY
MONDAY 16th MAY 7-30PM

MAY

THE CLASH'S FELLOW RIOTERS

The White Riot tour was also punk's first package tour, with The Clash headlining a bill of three other bands (four until The Jam pulled out after the first week). Buzzcocks had regrouped after singer Howard Devoto left in March, with Pete Shelley and Steve Diggle now on guitar. Subway Sect, fronted by Vic Godard, were one of the first generation punk bands, appearing at the 100 Club Punk Special in 1976. They released a single, 'Nobody's Scared', and were managed by Clash manager Bernie Rhodes, who perversely sacked the band (apart from Godard) just after recording an album. The Slits (pictured above) were a female quartet playing virtually their first gigs on the tour. They faced sexist abuse from the audiences, but gave as good as they got.

MAY

THE SEX PISTOLS SIGN TO VIRGIN

On 12 May 1977 The Sex Pistols signed their third record contract in six months, this time with Virgin Records. It was an unexpected move because Virgin had a reputation as a hippie label and was threatened with extinction now that sales of Mike Oldfield's *TUBULAR BELLS* were tailing off. Within a year Virgin Records would be the go-to independent label of choice for aspiring punk and new wave bands. The Sex Pistols received an advance of £65,000 to add to the £125,000 they'd already received from EMI and A&M. And Virgin announced that the band's new single would be 'God Save The Queen'.

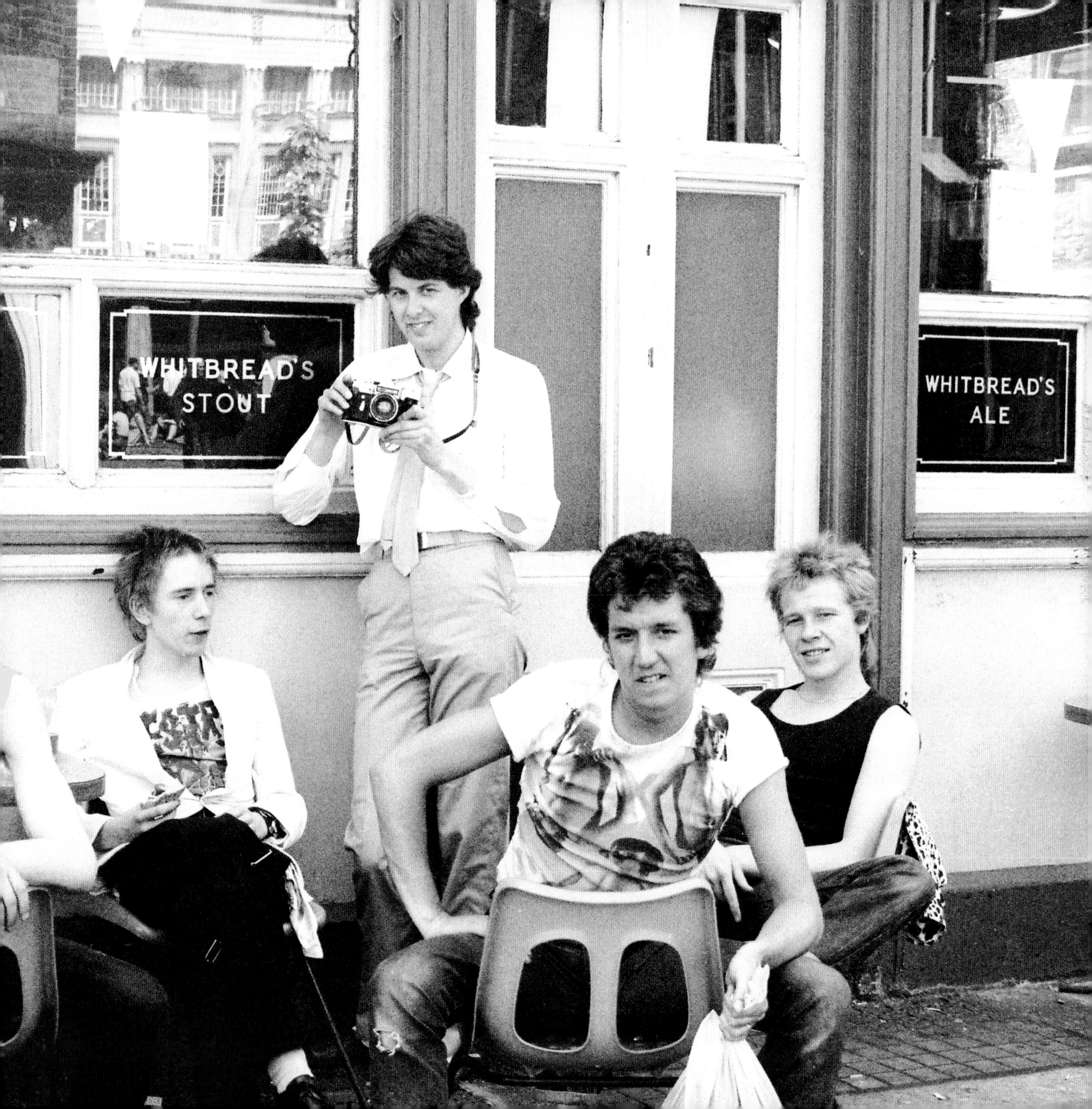
WHITBREAD'S
STOUT
WHITBREAD'S
ALE

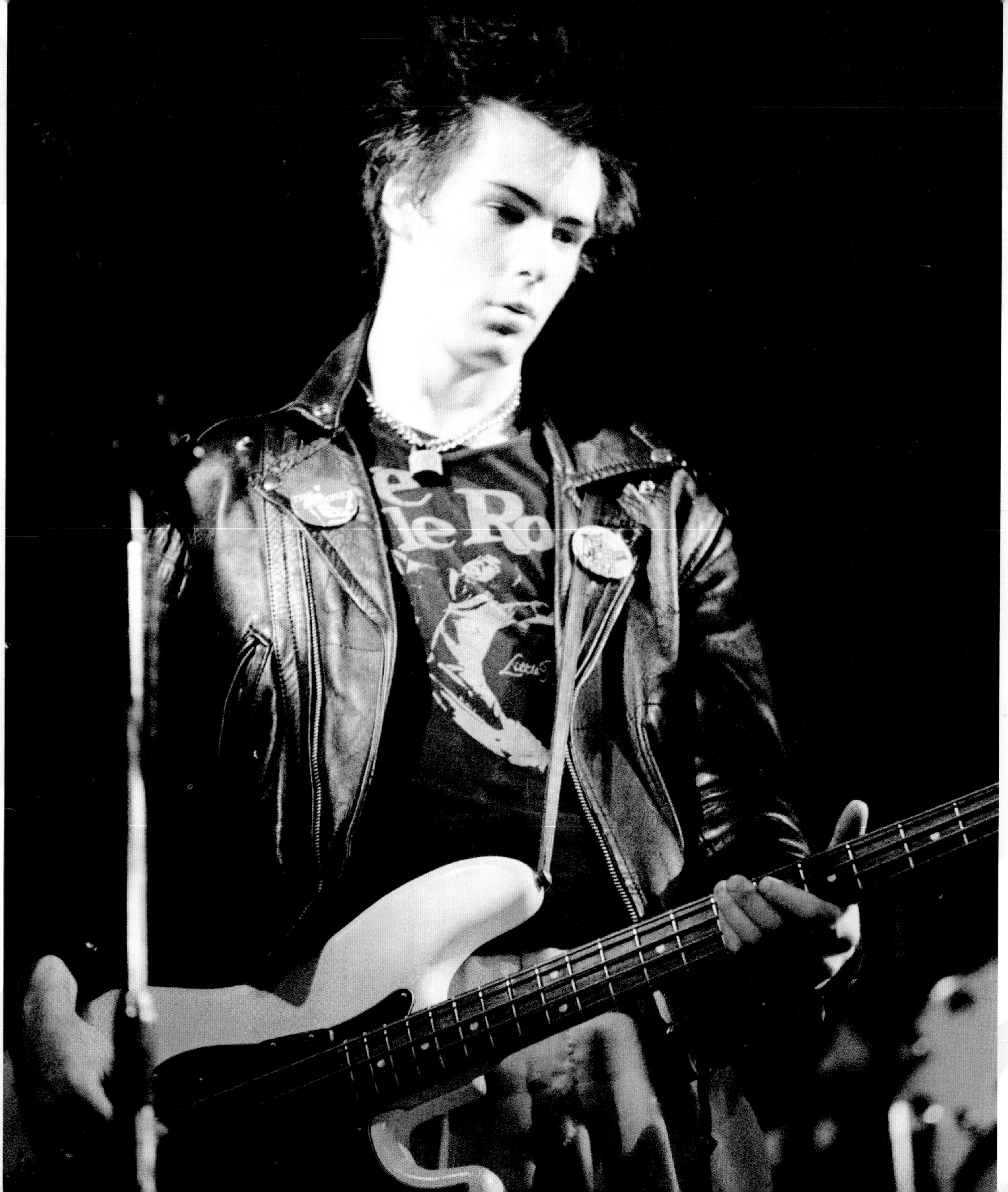

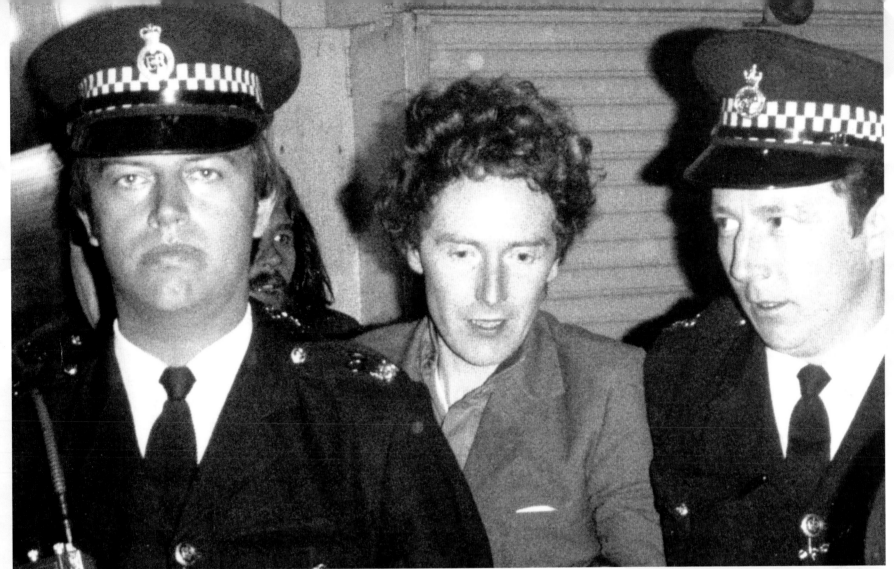

MAY

THE SEX PISTOLS' 'GOD SAVE THE QUEEN'

Released on 27 May 1977, a week before the official Silver Jubilee, 'God Save The Queen' became the symbol of British punk. It's not just the song that goes for the jugular – from the opening 'God save the Queen/ It's a fascist regime' to the closing snarl of 'No future' – it's also the cover design by Jamie Reid, featuring a defaced picture of Her Majesty. Although it almost certainly committed lese-majesty – the violation of the dignity of a reigning monarch – no charges were ever brought. The song was banned by the BBC and independent radio, but in its first week it is generally believed to have outsold its nearest rival, Rod Stewart's 'I Don't Want To Talk About It', by some margin, reportedly selling 150,000 copies in a single day. When the official chart was published, however, it was placed at No. 2. This discrepancy has never been acknowledged or explained.

JUNE

McLAREN MESSES ABOUT ON THE RIVER

On the day of the Silver Jubilee – 7 June 1977 – Malcolm McLaren hired a boat and took The Sex Pistols and invited guests on a river trip up the Thames. Aboard the aptly named Queen Elizabeth, the noisy party atmosphere increased as they passed the Houses of Parliament and the band played 'Anarchy In The UK'. They had already attracted the attention of the river police, who escorted them back to shore where the boat was boarded by the police. In the ensuing scuffles, 11 people were arrested, including McLaren.

PISTOL WHIPPING

In the days following The Sex Pistols' boat party, both Paul Cook and 'God Save The Queen' cover designer Jamie Reid were beaten up in unprovoked attacks on the street. Johnny Rotten was attacked twice in three days. However, sympathy for the group was limited because of the aura of violence that frequently surrounded their gigs. There were also instances of the band and their entourage engaging in violent altercations in pubs and clubs, sometimes provoked, sometimes not. Sid Vicious had been involved in several of these incidents and he was now in an abusive relationship with his girlfriend Nancy Spungen.

JUNE

SHEENA IS A HIT FOR THE RAMONES

Punk's transition from underground cult to the mainstream was clearly illustrated by The Ramones' 'Sheena Is A Punk Rocker', which reached No. 22 in the UK charts in June 1977 and No. 81 in the US. Joey Ramone described it as 'the first surf/punk rock/teenage rebellion song. I combined Sheena, Queen of the Jungle (a 1940s comic-book heroine) with the primalness of punk. Then Sheena is brought into the modern day.' At 2 minutes 45 seconds the song was an epic in Ramones terms. A year and a half after 'Blitzkrieg Bop' the tempo hadn't dropped but the production was cleaner, giving their sound even more power.

JUNE

MANIC VIBRATORS

One of the first generation of punk bands, The Vibrators survived the attentions of producer Mickie Most, who wanted to turn them into pop punks. They toured the UK with Iggy Pop and released their first album, PURE MANIA, in June 1977, camouflaging – but not submerging – their pop instincts in a barrage of relentless tempos and raw vocals, most notably on their 'Baby Baby' single. They also had wit, a rare punk commodity at that time. The underrated album briefly scraped into the UK Top 50, but it was more influential than that – Stiff Little Fingers took their name from an album track.

THE VIBRATORS

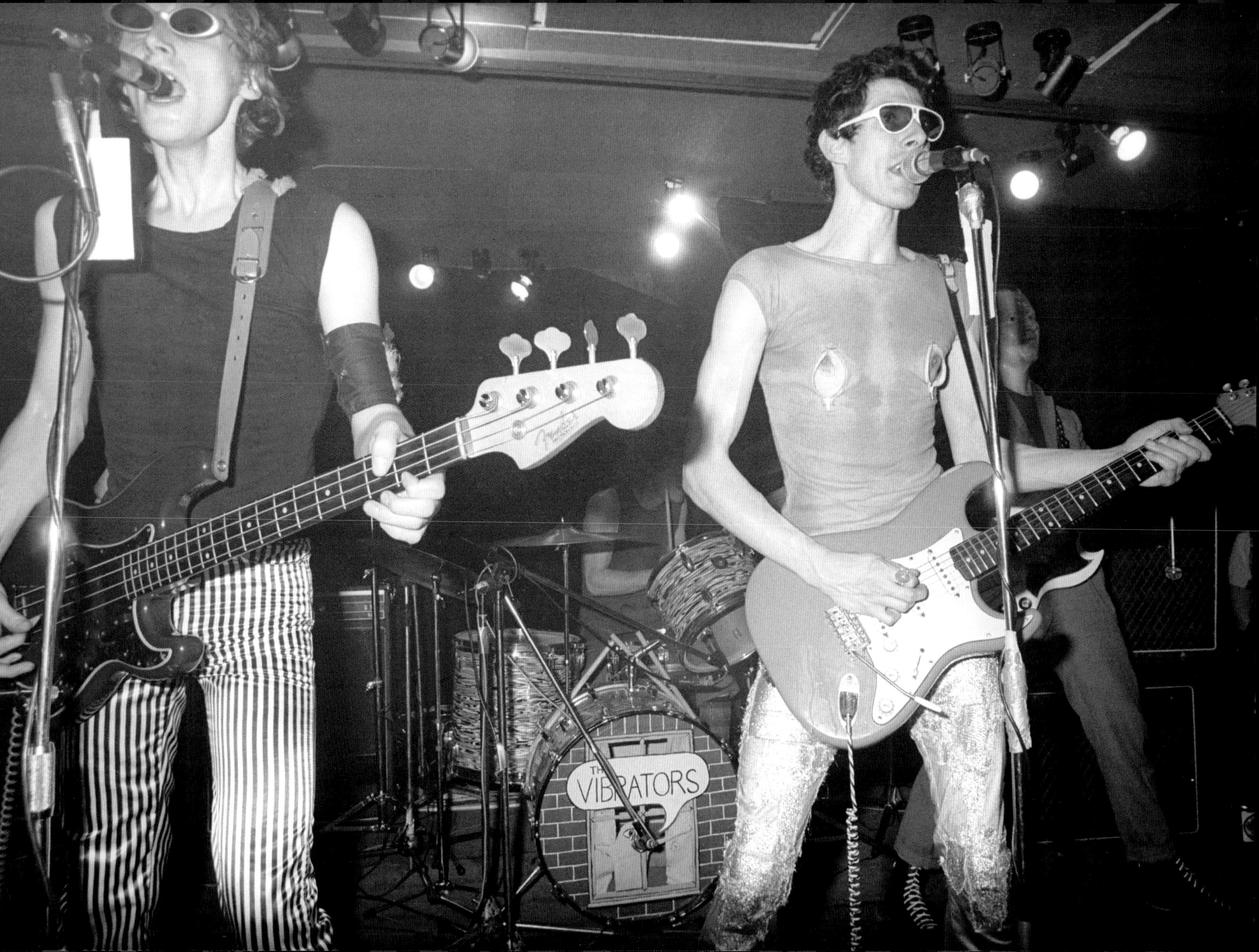

THE VIBRATORS

July

THE SEX PISTOLS' 'PRETTY VACANT'

If The Sex Pistols were finding it hard to walk down the street unmolested, or find a place to play, they could still roll out the punk anthems. 'Pretty Vacant', released on 1 July, was essentially a pop song formula (it was apparently written after hearing ABBA's 'SOS'). But once Steve Jones' blunt, resonating guitar and Johnny Rotten's acid lyrics got stuck into it, the song became something else entirely. The BBC, having checked carefully to make sure the song was neither seditious nor treasonable, invited the group to mime their single on *Top Of The Pops*. Unfortunately, they hadn't reckoned on Rotten's pronunciation of the word 'vacant' with its heavy emphasis on the second syllable.

AUSSIE PUNK

JULY

RADIO BIRDMAN APPEARS

Along with The Saints, Radio Birdman were among the most influential bands in the emerging Australian punk scene. They'd formed in Sydney in 1974, energized by MC5 and The Stooges. And if they hadn't been listening too closely (their name is a mis-hearing of The Stooges' lyric 'radio burnin'), they'd got the message. They developed their own underground scene around the Oxford Funhouse and followed the DIY route, releasing their **RADIOS APPEAR** album on an independent label in July 1977. It was ignored by commercial radio, even after WEA licensed the album. By the time Sire picked up the album a year later, the moment had gone.

THE AUSTRALIAN SCENE

The Australian punk scene produced some of the earliest punk music but remained fragmented because of the country's geography. Sydney was the notional centre with Radio Birdman and The Saints (who'd moved from Melbourne), soon joined by The Last Words (pictured opposite), formed by UK migrants Malcolm Baxter and Andy Groome. Their first single, 'Animal World', was so good they released it three times on three different labels. After The Saints left Melbourne, the scene was filled by Boys Next Door, featuring the young Nick Cave and Mick Harvey, who were on the fringes of glam before they heard The Saints' first album and became The Birthday Party. Across in Perth, The Victims launched a weekly punk night at a local club that featured The Cheap Nasties, who later became The Scientists.

JULY

THE SEX PISTOLS TOUR SCANDINAVIA

Finally The Sex Pistols found somewhere they could play –
Scandinavia. Malcolm McLaren lined up a two-week tour in
July, while he flew to Hollywood to talk movies with Russ Meyer.
The tour got off to an inauspicious start when Sid Vicious left
his passport behind and the first two Copenhagen gigs to an
audience seated at tables were plagued by sound problems.
The Swedish gigs went better, until they got to the God-fearing
town of Jönköping where the police rushed in and closed the
show after 20 minutes, citing a bomb scare. The Oslo show
in Norway was briefly halted after an ashtray was thrown at
Johnny Rotten.

VIVE LE PUNK

The second Mont de Marson punk festival in Southern France was staged in August, attracting a crowd of some 4,000 people to the town's bullfighting arena. Among the bands playing were The Clash, The Damned, The Slits, The Police, Dr Feelgood and The Tyla Gang, plus French bands Little Bob Story and Asphalt Jungle. The Clash (pictured opposite) took the opportunity to play a new song, '(White Man) In Hammersmith Palais', that merged punk and reggae rhythms for the first time. A week later, the band's headlining appearance at the Bilzen Festival in Belgium provoked a riot and Paul Simonon's bass amp was smashed by a flying brick.

THE SEX PISTOLS' SECRET TOUR

Fed up with not being able to play gigs in Britain because of their reputation, The Sex Pistols organized a series of dates under various pseudonyms. They started at Wolverhampton Lafayette on 19 August, billed as SPOTS (which stood for Sex Pistols On Tour Secretly). They then played Doncaster Outlook Club as The Tax Exiles, Scarborough as Special Guest, Middlesbrough as Acne Ramble, Plymouth as The Hamsters and Penzance as A Mystery Band Of International Repute. It worked. There were no serious incidents at any of the gigs, although the audience numbers were smaller than might have been expected.

THE ADVERTS MAKE EYE CONTACT

The Adverts had been building a reputation at London's
Roxy Club during 1977 with their two punk anthems, the self-
deprecating 'One Chord Wonders' and 'Bored Teenagers', and
their classic punk look, notably bassist Gaye Advert's jet-black
hair, black leather jacket and panda eyes. Their second single,
'Gary Gilmore's Eyes', a Top 20 hit in August of that year, was
written after convicted American murderer Gary Gilmore had
requested that his eyes be donated to medical science after
his execution. The song speculated what it would be like
'looking through Gary Gilmore's eyes'. Once the media had
got over the initial shock, they did acknowledge the perceptive
talents of singer and songwriter TV Smith.

X-RAY SEPX'S 'OH BONDAGE, UP YOURS!'

'Some people think little girls should be seen and not heard. But I say Oh Bondage, Up Yours!' declares Poly Styrene of X-Ray Spex, her voice rising to a screech on the band's first single, released in September 1977. And for the next two minutes she delivers a tirade of anti-sexism, anti-racism and anti-conformity above a barrage of chopping guitars and a saxophone, occasionally repeating the song title for emphasis. X-Ray Spex revelled in a riot of day-glo colours while Poly displayed her teeth braces at every opportunity and wore strange stiff plastic dresses. They were an instant favourite at London's Roxy club and a lot more than just a novelty act, as any passing journalist quickly found out.

YOUR GENERATION X

Guitarist Tony James (from the failed London SS group) and bassist Billy Idol were playing in Chelsea, led by singer Gene October, when they quit in late 1976 to form Generation X, with Billy Idol moving to vocals. They were the first band to play the Roxy and although their poppy punk sound and somewhat contrived image kept the sceptics scowling, they kept the record companies keen, eventually signing to Chrysalis and releasing their anthemic first single, 'Your Generation' in September 1977, which made the UK Top 40 and got them on to *Top Of The Pops*.

SEPTEMBER

GALLIC PUNK

French punk band Stinky Toys (pictured opposite), with high-pitched, fidgety girl singer Elli Medeiros, first came to London for the 100 Club Punk Festival in September 1976, although they didn't really mingle. They signed to Polydor in 1977 and released the first non-English punk single, the perky 'Boozy Creed', that September, but it raised little interest. Like many of the French punk bands of that era – Asphalt Jungle, Marie Et Les Garcons, Oberkampf and Starshooter – they focussed on the style rather than the substance. Metal Urbain were an exception, using a synthesizer and a drum machine (which solved the eternal punk drummer problem) that gave them an innovative musical style.

EURO PUNK

In the mid-1970s a German punk scene grew up in West Berlin, fuelled by the city's isolation and claustrophobia. It was centred around the SO36 Club, where David Bowie and Iggy Pop would hang out when in town, watching bands like PVC. There was also an early punk scene in Hamburg led by the aggressive Big Balls & The Great White Idiot, whose singer wore a Nazi uniform. Punk fans in Munich (like those pictured above) hung out at clubs like Schwabinger Brau and the Downtown Club and got to see The Clash, The Ramones and Blondie during 1977. In Switzerland, The Nasal Boys set the pace, supporting The Clash at their Zurich gig in 1977 and releasing the speedy 'Hot Love'. Behind them were all-girl avant-garde punkettes Fresh Color, featuring Dieter Maeier who would go on to form Yello. Provincial punk scenes also developed in Yugoslavia (as close as punk got to socialist countries), with Pankrti from Slovenia and Paraf from Croatia.

SEPTEMBER

THE CLASH TAKE CONTROL

Mid-way through The Clash's White Riot tour, CBS had issued a single, 'Remote Control', taken from their debut album, without telling the band. 'Complete Control' was The Clash's vitriolic response, released as a single in September 1977. The record company was happy to be the butt of the joke as long as the single was a hit, which it was. The song was produced by Jamaican reggae legend Lee 'Scratch' Perry, who had heard and admired The Clash's version of 'Police And Thieves', but the band sneaked in afterwards and turned down the echo and turned the guitars back up.

SEPTEMBER

THE VOIDOIDS' BLANK GENERATION

When Richard Hell released his own album, **BLANK GENERATION**, with his own band, The Voidoids, in September 1977, after abortive stints with Television and The Heartbreakers, it was easier to see why he'd teamed up with Television's Tom Verlaine in the first place. They both shared an edgy musical tension and literate lyrical sense. The difference was that Hell preferred to write songs with catchy hooks like the title track or 'Love Comes In Spurts', which revealed Hell to be something of a frustrated romantic, despite the song's title and Hell's iconic punk image.

SEPTEMBER

TALKING HEADS SPEAK UP

Having spent two years honing their act in New York's Bowery bars and dives, Talking Heads released their first album, 77, in September 1977. Their songs were itchy and compulsive, epitomized by the jerky, urgent 'Psycho Killer' that was carried along by bassist Tina Weymouth and drummer Chris Frantz. But in amongst the precision playing, the ingenious arrangements and singer/guitarist David Byrne's carefully enunciated lyrics there were intriguing song titles like 'Uh-Oh, Love Comes To Town' and 'Don't Worry About The Government', along with sardonic lines like 'They say compassion is a virtue but I don't have the time'. Plus a sense that this was all leading somewhere.

OCTOBER

THE HEARTBREAKERS' L.A.M.F.

Johnny Thunders & The Heartbreakers had taken up Malcolm McLaren's invitation to the UK in 1976. In return they have been credited with introducing heroin to the UK punk scene. They supported The Sex Pistols on their ill-fated Anarchy tour and signed to Track Records to record an album. They had some anthemic songs, notably Johnny Thunders' 'Chinese Rocks', an ode to his favourite brand of smack. But the problems came when it got to the mixing stage. Each group member made their own mix and Track was left with 37 reels of tape to make an album from. The result was L.A.M.F., released in October 1977 – a big aural mess that even their fans could barely listen to. The band fell apart soon afterwards.

THE SEX PISTOLS ON HOLIDAY

The Sex Pistols' fourth single, 'Holidays In The Sun', came out in October, giving them their third Top 10 hit. It was written after the band's attempt at a holiday, when they'd been thrown off the island of Jersey and decamped to West Berlin. The riff was ripped off from The Jam's 'In The City'. At least that's what Sid Vicious told Paul Weller in London's Speakeasy Club. 'He just came up to me and he was going on about "Holidays In The Sun" where they'd nicked the riff from "In The City",' Weller told *Uncut* magazine. 'I didn't mind them nicking it – you've got to get your ideas from somewhere, haven't you? Anyway, he just came up and nutted me. So I returned it.' The sleeve design was ripped off from a Belgian Travel Service poster, which kept the lawyers busy.

THE DEAD BOYS GET LOUD AND SNOTTY

The Dead Boys pulled no punches on their debut album, starting with the title, **YOUNG, LOUD AND SNOTTY**, released in October 1977. But it was an articulate aural onslaught. Singer Stiv Bators snarled, gobbed and whined above the band's garage punk and distorted 1950s rock'n'roll, but they never lost sight of the song. And from the opening phased drums at the start of nailed-on classic 'Sonic Reducer', they would use any trick to make a song great. 'Ain't Nothing To Do' is brutish because that's the way they wanted it, not forgetting the filthy love ballad 'All This And More' and the self-explanatory 'Caught With The Meat In Your Mouth'.

OCTOBER

THE CLASH GET OUT OF CONTROL

Unlike The Sex Pistols, The Clash had no problems playing gigs. Their Get Out Of Control tour in October 1977 pulled in 22 dates in 25 days. At Dublin's Trinity College they were watched by two impressionable teenagers, later known as Bono and The Edge, who found it a life-changing experience. The last date in Manchester was filmed for Granada TV's *So It Goes*. Strummer dedicated 'I'm So Bored With The USA' to 'Ted Nugent, Aerosmith, Journey and, most of all, Blue Oyster Cult'. It so happened Blue Oyster Cult's manager/producer was in the audience and was in the frame to produce The Clash's next album.

OCTOBER

NEVER MIND THE PISTOLS

The Sex Pistols' eagerly awaited first album was released on 28 October 1977. NEVER MIND THE BOLLOCKS, HERE'S THE SEX PISTOLS was immediately banned for its title alone by Boots, WHSmith and Woolworths, along with a TV and radio advertising ban. None of which stopped the album from going to No. 1 in the UK. A Nottingham record shop owner who displayed the cover in the window was prosecuted for obscenity, together with Virgin Records' owner Richard Branson. Defending barrister John Mortimer produced expert witnesses to testify that 'bollocks' was not an obscenity, but an Old English term meaning 'nonsense'. The magistrates reluctantly dismissed the charges. The album, which featured the first four Sex Pistols' singles, sold poorly outside the UK and Europe, but has since figured in virtually every list of 'best albums' ever published.

NOVEMBER

THE RAMONES' ROCKET TO RUSSIA

With their third album, **ROCKET TO RUSSIA**, The Ramones achieved the perfect blend of garage surf music and minimalist punk, epitomized by 'Sheena Is A Punk Rocker' and 'Rockaway Beach'. They also covered The Trashmen's 'Surfin' Bird' and Bobby Freeman's 'Do You Wanna Dance?', a hit for The Beach Boys. The album, which also included 'Teenage Lobotomy' and 'Cretin Hop', was the first to crack the US Top 50. After the album's release on 4 November 1977, drummer and co-producer Tommy Ramone left the group, although he continued to manage and produce them. His replacement, Voidoids drummer Marc Bell, changed his name to Marky Ramone for The Ramones European tour. Their London Rainbow Theatre concert was recorded for **IT'S ALIVE**, eventually released in 1979.

NOVEMBER

DARK SIDE OF THE DAMNED

Having taken the inexplicable decision to hire Pink Floyd drummer Nick Mason to produce their second album, The Damned proceeded to have musical differences of their own in the studio. Guitarist and main songwriter Brian James, who had recently recruited fellow guitarist Lu Edmunds to fill out the sound, wanted to progress while the others wanted more of the same. The result was, as one of the tracks had it, a 'Stretcher Case'. **MUSIC FOR PLEASURE** was disowned by the band and the public when it was released in November 1977. Rat Scabies had already left, James soon followed to form Tanz Der Youth and The Damned looked doomed. But a few months later, Scabies was back with Dave Vanian and Captain Sensible for reunion shows without James.

DECEMBER

THE SEX PISTOLS BEAT THE BANS

After the furore surrounding **NEVER MIND THE BOLLOCKS, HERE'S THE SEX PISTOLS** a Never Mind The Bans UK club tour was set up for mid-December. There was resistance from the Methodist venue owners in Rochdale and the Bristol Bamboo Club burnt down the day before the scheduled gig, but other provincial dates including Coventry, Keighley, Wolverhampton and Cromer went ahead without problems. The last date of the tour was at Ivanhoe's, Huddersfield, on Christmas Day. The band played two shows, the first in aid of 'striking firemen, laid-off workers and one-parent families'. It was the last time The Sex Pistols played in the UK.

1978

JANUARY

THE SEX PISTOLS HEAD SOUTH

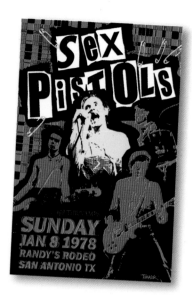

At the beginning of January 1978 The Sex Pistols flew out to Atlanta, Georgia, for a series of dates in the American South. It all unravelled at Randy's Rodeo in San Antonio on 8 January in front of 2,000 rowdy Texans: Sid Vicious was suffering from heroin withdrawal and behaving aggressively; Rotten's T-shirt depicting two homosexual cowboys was not received well; and Steve Jones and Paul Cook struggled to hold the show together against a barrage of food and plastic cups. Over the next three shows in Baton Rouge, Dallas and Tulsa the band effectively disintegrated as Vicious's behaviour worsened – he had scrawled 'Gimme a fix' across his chest and was picking fights at every opportunity.

JANUARY

FINALE FOR THE PISTOLS

What could have been The Sex Pistols' first proper American show at San Francisco's Winterland Ballroom on 14 January in front of 5,000 people, including a sizeable punk contingent, was instead an incoherent, dispirited shambles. Sid Vicious was barely conscious, Johnny Rotten was alert but deliberately uninvolved, while Steve Jones and Paul Cook just couldn't be bothered. There was no musical spirit between them. At the end of the encore, appropriately a cover of The Stooges' 'No Fun', Rotten glared at the audience and snarled 'Ever had the feeling you've been cheated?' before walking off. For him it was all over.

JANUARY

THE PISTOLS FADE INTO FARCE

It was Johnny Rotten who announced the band's demise after he'd flown to New York and before he realized he didn't have enough money to get back to Britain. Sid Vicious had also flown to New York to get detox treatment in hospital. Seemingly oblivious to the realities around him, Malcolm McLaren was making it up as he went along, flying Steve Jones and Paul Cook down to Rio de Janeiro to goof around with fugitive British train robber Ronald Biggs, luring Vicious to Paris to film a barrel-scraping version of 'My Way', all of which would turn up on the aptly named GREAT ROCK'N'ROLL SWINDLE movie.

FEBRUARY

THE ADVERTS CROSS THE RED SEA

They may have progressed from simplistic 'One Chord Wonders' to the more complex 'Gary Gilmore's Eyes', but The Adverts never lost sight of their basic, distinctive style on their first album, CROSSING THE RED SEA WITH THE ADVERTS, released in February 1978. TV Smith had a melodic snarl that made his lyrics stand out and his songs encompassed teen anthems like 'Bored Teenagers' and 'No Time To Be 21' along with broader, socially aware songs like 'Bombsite Boys'. They knew how to make their musical limitations work for them, as bassist and punk dreamboat Gaye Advert powerfully displayed on 'Safety In Numbers'. Guitarist Howard Pickup kept his solos short and sharp and drummer Laurie Driver could handle a range of tempos. Green Day are just one band to acknowledge the influence of that album.

FEBRUARY

SHAM 69 BREAK OUT

Sham 69's brand of working-class suburban punk, with its defiantly rabble-rousing slogans, shook up the scene during the latter part of 1977. Fronted by the charismatic Jimmy Pursey, they chalked up a series of hits such as 'Borstal Breakout', 'Angels With Dirty Faces', 'If The Kids Were United' and 'Hurry Up Harry'. First album TELL US THE TRUTH was released on 18 February 1978. They attracted a strong skinhead following that packed out the Roxy and other punk clubs like the Vortex. But the skinheads did not mingle easily with the punks and there were inevitable associations with the extreme right-wing National Front. Sham 69 were vehemently anti-racist but Pursey found it hard to reason with his followers and their gigs were increasingly marred by violence and intimidation.

MARCH

BUZZCOCKS COME OUT OF THE KITCHEN

One of the first wave of British punk bands, Buzzcocks had to reconfigure themselves after singer Howard Devoto left in early 1977. The new front pairing of angelic, ambiguous Pete Shelley and the mod-looking Steve Diggle seemed incongruous, but they turned out to be the perfect foil for each other. Their first single, 'Orgasm Addict', was a comment on punk's reluctance to talk about sex, but it was banned by the BBC. Their first album, **ANOTHER MUSIC IN A DIFFERENT KITCHEN**, released in March 1978, was packed with clever pop songs using riffs from the Stooges to T. Rex with lyrics of doomed romanticism that echoed John Lennon and Ray Davies at their finest.

APRIL

THE CLASH ROCK AGAINST RACISM

The rise of the National Front in the mid-1970s had provoked the formation of Rock Against Racism to counter the political apathy among young people that was playing into the hands of right-wing extremists. A Rock Against Racism concert was organized at East London's Victoria Park on 30 April 1978 and The Clash headlined a bill that included Steel Pulse, Sham 69, Generation X, X-Ray Spex and The Tom Robinson Band. It was the biggest gig The Clash had ever played, in front of an estimated 80,000 people, at which they debuted a new song, 'English Civil War', about the dangers of right-wing politics. It was a defining moment for anti-racism in Britain as well as The Clash. It was also a defining moment in the decline of the National Front.

JUNE

MUSICAL DEPARTURE FOR THE CLASH

With the release of '(White Man) In Hammersmith Palais' on 17 June 1978, The Clash demonstrated a new versatility. It was written by Joe Strummer after he'd been to a reggae all-nighter at London's Hammersmith Palais that left him feeling disillusioned. He took out his disappointment on the state of the nation in general and the state of punk rock in particular. Musically it was also something of a departure for The Clash, moving away from their strident riffing style into slower ska-based rhythms. It had few of the attributes associated with a conventional single, but such was the growing popularity of The Clash that it got to No. 32 in the UK chart that summer.

JULY

THE CLASH OUT ON PAROLE

The Clash headed out on their Out On Parole tour during July 1978, playing 26 shows in 30 days, including four nights at London's Camden Music Machine. They premiered several new songs, and paid homage to The Ramones with a version of 'Blitzkrieg Bop', as well as flexing their reggae rhythms with '(White Man) In Hammersmith Palais' and Junior Murvin's 'Police And Thieves'. The tour's title referred to The Clash's numerous run-ins with the police: Paul Simonon and Topper Headon had been arrested after shooting at pigeons from a studio roof; while Joe Strummer and Mick Jones had been fined for stealing a pillowcase from a Newcastle hotel. During the tour, Jones was busted in Blackburn while Strummer and Simonon were arrested and fined for being drunk and disorderly in Glasgow.

AUGUST

SIOUXSIE'S GARDEN PARTY

As part of the Bromley Contingent, Siouxsie and her mates – some of whom became Banshees – had a front-row seat for the first wave of punk in 1976. But it was another two years before Siouxsie & The Banshees got to release their first single. 'Hong Kong Garden', which came out in August 1978, was dedicated to their local Chinese restaurant where the staff were routinely racially abused by local skinheads. The song, which featured oriental guitar riffs and a distinctive drum sound, was a Top 10 hit, reaching No. 7 in the UK chart. It was also a first hit record for producer Steve Lillywhite.

SEPTEMBER

BUZZCOCKS FALL IN LOVE AGAIN

Buzzcocks' skill at crafting quirky love songs out of frenzied punk was brilliantly demonstrated on 'Ever Fallen In Love (With Someone You Shouldn't've)', which reached No. 12 in the UK singles charts in September 1978. The title came from the dialogue of the *Guys And Dolls* movie that they'd watched on TV one night on tour, and Pete Shelley's lyrics were driven by drummer John Mayer's relentless rhythm and a couple of unusual chord changes. The song was taken from their second album, **LOVE BITES**, released the same month, that took a pop slant on punk with its tight, twin guitar attack and sparse riffs. It worked so well that the band found themselves being screamed rather than gobbed at.

SEPTEMBER

THE RAMONES ON THE ROAD TO RUIN

After four albums in two years, there were signs that The Ramones' formula was starting to wear a little thin. ROAD TO RUIN, released in September 1978, sounded forced in places and the album had neither the exuberant energy nor the array of hooks that had characterized the previous three. Ironically, the best song came when they slowed down the tempo for 'I Wanna Be Sedated'. Songs like 'Don't Come Close' and a cover of Jackie De Shannon's 'Needles And Pins' suggested that 'Da Brudders' had given up surf punk in favour of 1960s girlie pop.

OCTOBER

FROM ROTTEN TO LYDON

While Malcolm McLaren was trying to reinvent the legend of The Sex Pistols while the corpse was still warm, Johnny Rotten was getting on with his life. Changing his name back to John Lydon and resisting Virgin Records' boss Richard Branson's attempts to team him up with American punk band Devo, Lydon formed a band with his old school mate Jah Wobble, who promised to learn to play bass, and guitarist Keith Levene, who had played in an early line-up of The Clash. Lydon named the band Public Image Ltd (pictured above) and they released their self-titled single in October 1978, which was a UK Top 10 hit. Meanwhile Lydon's lawyers were building a case against McLaren.

OCTOBER

ELVIS COSTELLO'S RADIO TIRADE

When Elvis Costello was booked on the US TV show *Saturday Night Live* in December 1977 as a late replacement for The Sex Pistols when their visas had not come through in time, he was instructed by his record company, CBS, to perform 'Less Than Zero'. However, on air he broke off after a few bars to play 'Radio Radio' instead, a song lambasting the cosy relationship between radio and record companies that effectively controlled what people could hear. It was inspired in part by the UK ban on The Sex Pistols' 'God Save The Queen'. Costello's impromptu performance earned him a ban that wasn't lifted until 1989. 'Radio Radio' was released as a single in the UK in October 1978 and made the Top 30. It was never released as a single in the US.

NOVEMBER

THE POLICE ON THE BEAT

The Police lost what little punk credibility they'd had when they replaced guitarist Henry Padovani with ageing hippie Andy Summers. He'd heard Sting's songs and was enthused by their vitality. Early in 1978 they started recording an album without a record deal in place and in April A&M Records decided to take a punt on a song called 'Roxanne'. It failed to register but they had more success with 'Can't Stand Losing You', which hovered just outside the UK Top 40. Encouraged, they released The Police's first album, OUTLANDOS D'AMOUR, on 2 November 1978. Word spread slowly, but in April 1979 'Roxanne' suddenly clicked and reached No. 12 in the chart.

NOVEMBER

THE CLASH ON A ROPE

The Clash took the controversial decision to work with American producer Sandy Pearlman for their second album. Released on 10 November 1978, the result was a cleaner, harder, more powerful sound. There were accusations of 'selling out' but that didn't stop the album from reaching No. 2 in the UK charts. GIVE 'EM ENOUGH ROPE was a direct reflection of The Clash's world at the time they were making it: 'Safe European Home' caught the strangeness of being in Jamaica where they'd been sent to write songs; 'Guns On The Roof' took Paul Simonon and Topper Headon's pigeon-shooting escapade as a starting point; while 'Julie's Been Working For The Drug Squad' referenced a recent LSD factory bust in Wales. It was the first Clash album to be released in America, but it failed to make the US Top 100.

THE CLASH

THE CLASH SORT IT OUT

The Clash headed out on another lengthy UK tour in November 1978. The Sort It Out tour – so called after the band had parted company with manager Bernie Rhodes – covered some 35 dates, although several were cancelled by the local authorities fearing punk riots in their towns. The Glasgow Strathclyde shows were also cancelled by the band when they found admission was restricted to students. The tour included a benefit gig for Sid Vicious – now out on bail in New York charged with the murder of his girlfriend Nancy Spungen – at London's Camden Music Machine and finished with three nights at London's Lyceum Ballroom.

THE CLASH GO GIRL CRAZY

Supporting The Clash on their Sort It Out tour were The Slits (pictured opposite) and The Innocents, two predominantly female bands. The Slits had supported The Clash on their White Riot tour in 1977, but had yet to release a record. They had recorded a John Peel session in 1977 featuring their rough and ready reggae rhythms and quirky vocals. Six of the seven songs would eventually appear on their first album, *CUT*, released in September 1979, produced by Dennis Bovell. The Innocents could trace their roots back to The Flowers Of Romance, who had also spawned The Slits. They never released a record despite recording tracks for an EP with Sex Pistols' sound man Dave Goodman.

NOVEMBER

X-RAY SPEX GO GERM FREE

X-Ray Spex may have looked and sounded like a punk novelty act, but behind their garish costumes and singer Poly Styrene's screeching voice was a strong anti-consumerist theme that prevailed on **GERM FREE ADOLESCENTS**, issued in November 1978. Styrene's lyrics stressed the dehumanizing effects of modern society in general and the exploitation of women by major corporations in particular, backed by strong guitars and wild saxophone interjections. Two of the songs – 'The Day The World Turned Day-Glo' and 'Identity' – were Top 30 singles in the UK, while the album's title track made the Top 20. A two-week residency at New York's CBGBs could have been the start of an American breakthrough, except that the album wasn't released there and Styrene quit in 1979, eventually joining the Hare Krishna movement.

DECEMBER

PiL'S FIRST ISSUE

Having set the bar high with 'Public Image', John Lydon's Public Image Ltd – or PiL as they became known – pointed the post-punk way forward with their debut album, **FIRST ISSUE**, released in the UK in December 1978. The album was a mash-up of dub, progressive rock and various noises that showed glimpses of what would become acid rock. Guitarist Keith Levene came into his own as a foil for Lydon's anguished, disillusioned lyrics. Jah Wobble had fulfilled his promise to learn the bass guitar to thunderous effect – so loud that the band's US label Warner Brothers refused to release it until it had been mixed lower, and even then they didn't.

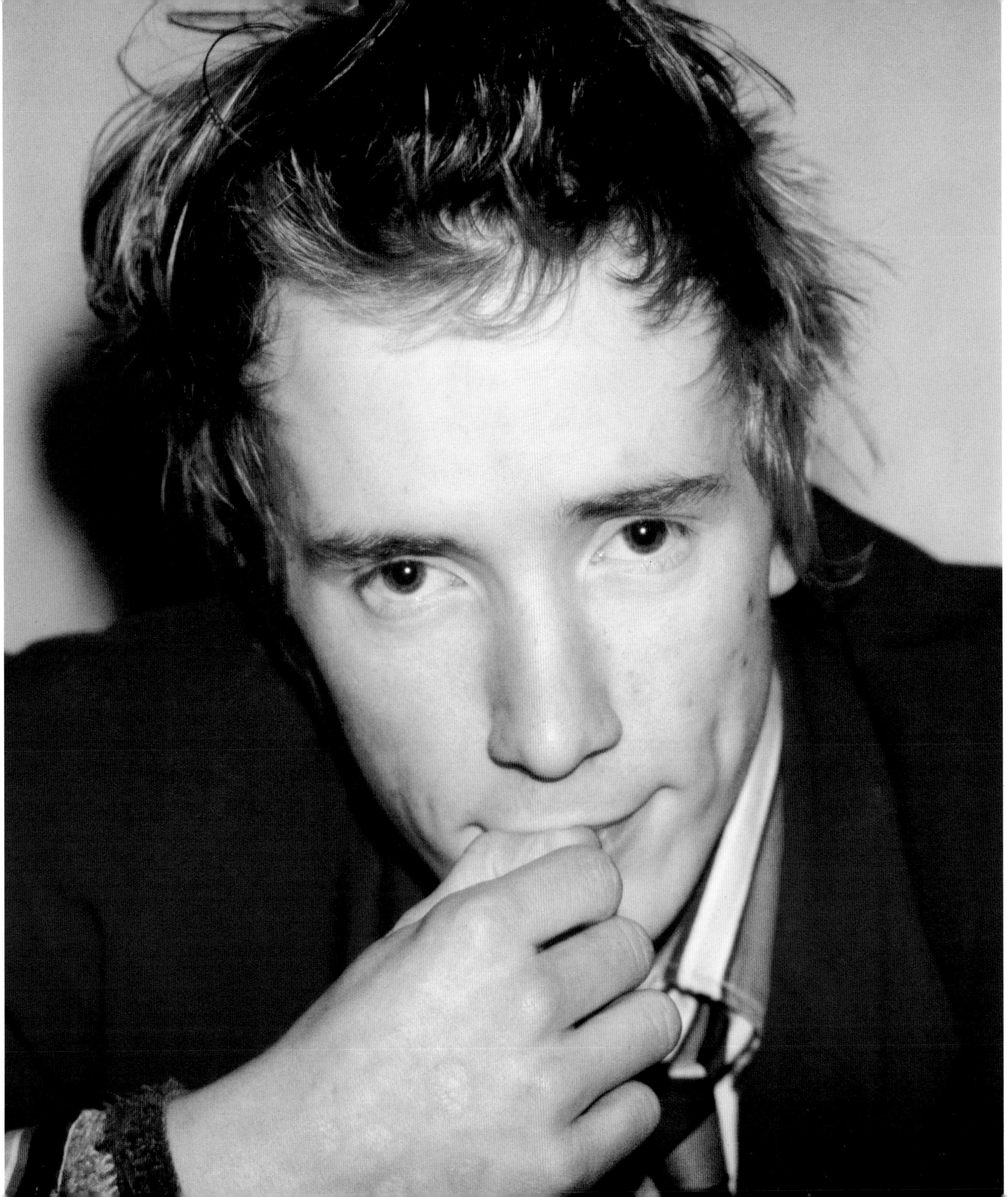

THE AFTERMATH: 1979 & BEYOND

1979 & BEYOND

Punk was pronounced dead on many occasions, as early as 1977 when The Clash signed to CBS and when The Sex Pistols split up the following year. By 1979 there was a consensus that, although the original impetus had died down, a thriving post-punk environment had arisen. Liverpool spawned the new psychedelia of Echo & The Bunnymen and The Teardrop Explodes. In the West Midlands, punk attitude fused with ska rhythms to produce two tone. New wave took the movement's vigour and applied a less uncompromising, more radio-friendly approach.

In America, the punk scene was an underground phenomenon, yet the influence of the bands who originated hardcore – The Dead Kennedys, Black Flag – would resonate down the years. Punk began to divide into sub-genres: anarcho-punk, no wave, Oi and punk-pop all changed the blueprint in strikingly different ways.

For some, punk was represented by a set of certain musical conventions and a rigid dress code, but in its purest form, punk was a movement for change. It challenged the musical establishment. It wasn't interested in standing still and repeating the same tired gestures. The aftershocks of punk would continue to be felt throughout the 1980s and 1990s; indie and alternative rock moved beyond their DIY origins and into the mainstream. More than 35 years on, punk is still alive and kicking down doors.

1979

JANUARY

IAN DURY'S RHYTHM STICK HITS NO. 1

An unlikely punk, Ian Dury was 35 when his first solo single, the anthemic 'Sex And Drugs And Rock And Roll', was released. A childhood polio victim, Dury had previously led pub rockers Kilburn & The High Roads. The album

NEW BOOTS AND PANTIES made him an equally unlikely star, taking up a lengthy residency in the chart. Recruiting The Blockheads allowed Dury to expand his musical palette to jazz and funk as a backdrop to his distinctive, often bawdy wordplay. 'Hit Me With Your Rhythm Stick' ascended to the top of the charts in January 1979 and represents the peak of his popularity.

FEBRUARY

SID VICIOUS FOUND DEAD

Sid Vicious was in New York trying to get a solo career together. He played three solo shows in the city in September, but his efforts were undermined by heroin addiction. Sid and girlfriend Nancy Spungen were staying at the notorious Chelsea Hotel when Spungen's body was found in a pool of blood on the morning of 12 October 1978. Emerging from a drugged stupor, Sid could not recall what happened. He was arrested for murder and sent to Rikers Island prison. After being bailed then re-arrested after a fight, a cleaned-up Sid was again released. He attended a celebratory party on the evening of 1 February 1979 where a fatal heroin overdose was administered, allegedly by his mother.

nycpd
m 4334003
12 8 78

STIFF LITTLE FINGERS IGNITE
INFLAMMABLE MATERIAL

English punks had long been moaning about boredom and disaffection, but their Northern Irish counterparts really did have grounds to complain. The presence of the British army and the ongoing Troubles created an environment that was dangerous and heavily restricted. Belfast's Stiff Little Fingers were a rock covers band until they discovered punk. At the suggestion of journalist (and later co-writer) Gordon Ogilvie, they began to write about the situation in Northern Ireland. John Peel's championing of their debut single 'Suspect Device' led to independent label Rough Trade signing the band. Debut album INFLAMMABLE MATERIAL, released on 2 February 1979, was a landmark, the first independent LP to chart in the UK.

THE CLASH INVADE AMERICA

The Clash had a complex relationship with America. 'I'm So Bored With The USA' was seen as an important part of their early manifesto. Their debut album was not deemed fit for American release until July 1979, and then in substantially altered form. The band's first assault on the States, the provocatively named Pearl Harbour tour, went ahead in February 1979 with less than enthusiastic record company backing. Nevertheless, The Clash performed a series of sold-out gigs. Highlights were a barnstorming show in Santa Monica and a triumphant night at the New York Palladium attended by the city's cognoscenti, including Andy Warhol and Bob Dylan.

FEBRUARY

McLAREN'S GREAT ROCK'N'ROLL SWINDLE

Malcolm McLaren's fictionalized film version of The Sex Pistols' story was finally released in May 1980, more than a year after the soundtrack album. The double set was a motley collection of new songs, demos, out-takes, rehearsals and cover versions, some not featuring The Pistols at all. Johnny Rotten declined to participate but his voice was heard, notably on an hilarious rehearsal of 'Johnny B. Goode'/ 'Roadrunner'. Elsewhere vocals were handled by Steve Jones, Paul Cook, Sid Vicious, McLaren himself and Great Train Robber Ronnie Biggs, who sang two songs. Amongst the non-Sex Pistols tracks was a disco medley of greatest hits by Black Arabs. The word 'swindle' seemed apposite.

LOVE THE DAMNED

The Damned were first with everything: the first punk single and album; the first punk band to split and the first to reform. After playing some reunion shows, they regrouped minus original guitarist and songwriter Brian James. Captain Sensible switched to guitar and ex-Saint Algy Ward was recruited on bass. The first fruits of a new record deal with independent label Chiswick was 'Love Song', released in April 1979 – a frenetically commercial tune, which gave them their first Top 20 hit. The single came in four different picture sleeves, each featuring a different band member, with 20,000 copies on collectable red vinyl.

APRIL

THE DICKIES DO THE SPLITS

It was generally seen as a good wheeze to give an old song the punk treatment by speeding it up and garbling the vocals. California's Dickies were notorious for performing this trick on many defenceless tunes, although they did produce their own material too. Fondly remembered by many punks, *Banana Splits* was a zany kids' magazine show from America, which aired in Britain in the late 1960s. The insanely catchy theme tune, also known as 'The Tra La La Song', became a football terrace chant before The Dickies took it into the UK Top 10 in April 1979. Social comment was not on the agenda.

BLONDIE AND THE NEW WAVE BOMBSHELLS

Although sometimes used as a polite synonym for punk, new wave is usually applied to bands with greater crossover appeal who came to prominence after the original momentum of punk had stalled. New wave was generally more polished and commercial but could still have an experimental edge, as exemplified by Talking Heads. In Britain, Elvis Costello perhaps best fitted the bill. Back in the USA, Blondie emerged from the New York scene to become the biggest new wave band of the immediate post-punk era. Debbie Harry's iconic looks and the hit single 'Heart Of Glass', which topped the *Billboard* chart in April 1979, helped catapult them into the big leagues.

JUNE

THE DEAD KENNEDYS ÜBER ALLES

According to singer Jello Biafra, his band's confrontational name was not an insult to the Kennedy dynasty, but a reference to the death of the American dream. The band was nevertheless often forced to perform under pseudonyms after forming in San Francisco early in 1978. Their first single, 'California Über Alles', was an effortlessly controversial debut released in June 1979. Biafra sneers his tale of then-governor of California Jerry Brown fantasizing about presiding over a totalitarian America under his laid-back 'zen fascist' regime. The singer later entered politics, running for mayor of San Francisco but finishing fourth.

JUNE

INTO THE UNKNOWN WITH JOY DIVISION

Manchester's thriving post-punk scene produced Joy Division, destined to become one of the most influential bands of the era. Their rise to greatness began when **UNKNOWN PLEASURES** was greeted with unanimous acclaim in the British music press. Released on 14 June 1979 through local independent label Factory Records, the first pressing ran to a modest 10,000 copies, which quickly sold out. The band was initially less than pleased by the stark, spacious ambience given to their music by legendary producer Martin Hannett, deeming it unrepresentative of their hard-hitting live sound. They have since revised that opinion as, over the years, **UNKNOWN PLEASURES** has retained its air of imposing mystery whilst gaining classic status.

JULY

THE CRAMPS' GRAVEST HITS

The core of The Cramps, husband-and-wife duo Lux Interior and Poison Ivy, remained constant whilst the rest of the line-up shifted around them. Their high-camp fusion of garage rock and rockabilly with retro B-movie sci-fi and horror was instrumental in creating psychobilly and, although The Cramps coined the term, they were quick to distance themselves from the genre. Nevertheless, many regard The Cramps' **GRAVEST HITS** EP as the first psychobilly record. The five-track 12-inch EP, released in July 1979, was a compilation of their first two independent singles, produced by former Big Star leader Alex Chilton.

SEPTEMBER

BUZZCOCKS FEEL THE TENSION

The third and final album from the 1970s incarnation of Buzzcocks was **A DIFFERENT KIND OF TENSION**, released in September 1979. The album was a schizophrenic affair, divided into two sides of contrasting material. The first featured relatively straightforward pop-punk (although the single 'You Say You Don't Love Me' flopped). Side two was given over to darker, more experimental material, which betrayed major songwriter Pete Shelley's clinically depressed state of mind. The album failed to match the impact of its two predecessors, and an untimely reminder of past glories in the shape of a singles and B-sides compilation, **GOING STEADY**, was released in America at the same time (two years later in the UK), coinciding with the group's first visit there.

SEPTEMBER

IGGY POP'S NEW VALUES

One of the godfathers of punk, Iggy Pop returned to recording in the movement's Year Zero, 1977, collaborating with David Bowie on **THE IDIOT** and **LUST FOR LIFE**. **NEW VALUES**, released in September 1979, saw Iggy revert to a fan-pleasing hard rock sound, with former Stooge James Williamson producing and playing guitar and touring Stooges member Scott Thurston

LET THE GANG OF FOUR ENTERTAIN YOU

Perhaps the archetypal British post-punk band, Gang Of Four's influence was to stretch far beyond the limited lifespan of their original incarnation. Formed in Leeds by singer Jon King, guitarist Andy Gill, bassist Dave Allen and drummer Hugo Burnham, their sound was a sparse mix of punk, funk and dub reggae set to politically aware lyrics. The first single from September 1979's ironically entitled **ENTERTAINMENT!**, 'At Home He's A Tourist', was chart bound until the band refused to change a reference to condoms and forfeited a *Top Of The Pops* appearance. The Gang Of Four split after 1981's **SOLID GOLD** and have reformed several times since.

THE POLICE'S REGATTA DE BLANC

Belated chart entries for 'Roxanne' and 'Can't Stand Losing You' in 1979 paved the way for the phenomenal success of **REGATTA DE BLANC**, The Police's second album, released in October of that year. Like its predecessor, the album boasted a cod-French title, a reference to the band's white reggae which, when fused with new wave rock, created their distinctive style. **REGATTA DE BLANC** and its two singles 'Message In A Bottle' and 'Walking On The Moon' were all chart toppers, establishing The Police as one of the UK's biggest groups. Nevertheless, they remained outsiders, regarded with suspicion by many of their new wave contemporaries.

THE DAMNED GUNNING FOR GLORY

The renaissance of The Damned continued apace. Hot on the heels of 'Love Song' was another classic single 'Smash It Up!' in September 1979, which entertainingly reworked punk ideology. Two months later came the first album by the reformed outfit, **MACHINE GUN ETIQUETTE**. The absence of former chief songwriter Brian James saw the credits shared more equally and their work now embraced psychedelia, garage rock and straight pop alongside their trademark punk energy. The album was generously received by the critics and is regarded as a major influence on gothic rock.

PIL BOX

METAL BOX was one of the most challenging and radical albums of the immediate post-punk era. The debut by John Lydon's new band Public Image Limited had been relatively accessible, albeit bearing little resemblance to The Sex Pistols. However, their second album forged a new direction. Relentlessly avant-garde and experimental, **METAL BOX** fused Keith Levene's ringing guitar, played on an aluminium instrument, Jah Wobble's dub reggae basslines and Lydon's anguished wail. The original packaging was equally uncompromising, consisting of three 12-inch 45-rpm records housed in a metal film can. Originally released on 23 November 1979, it was later reissued as a conventional double album, **SECOND EDITION**.

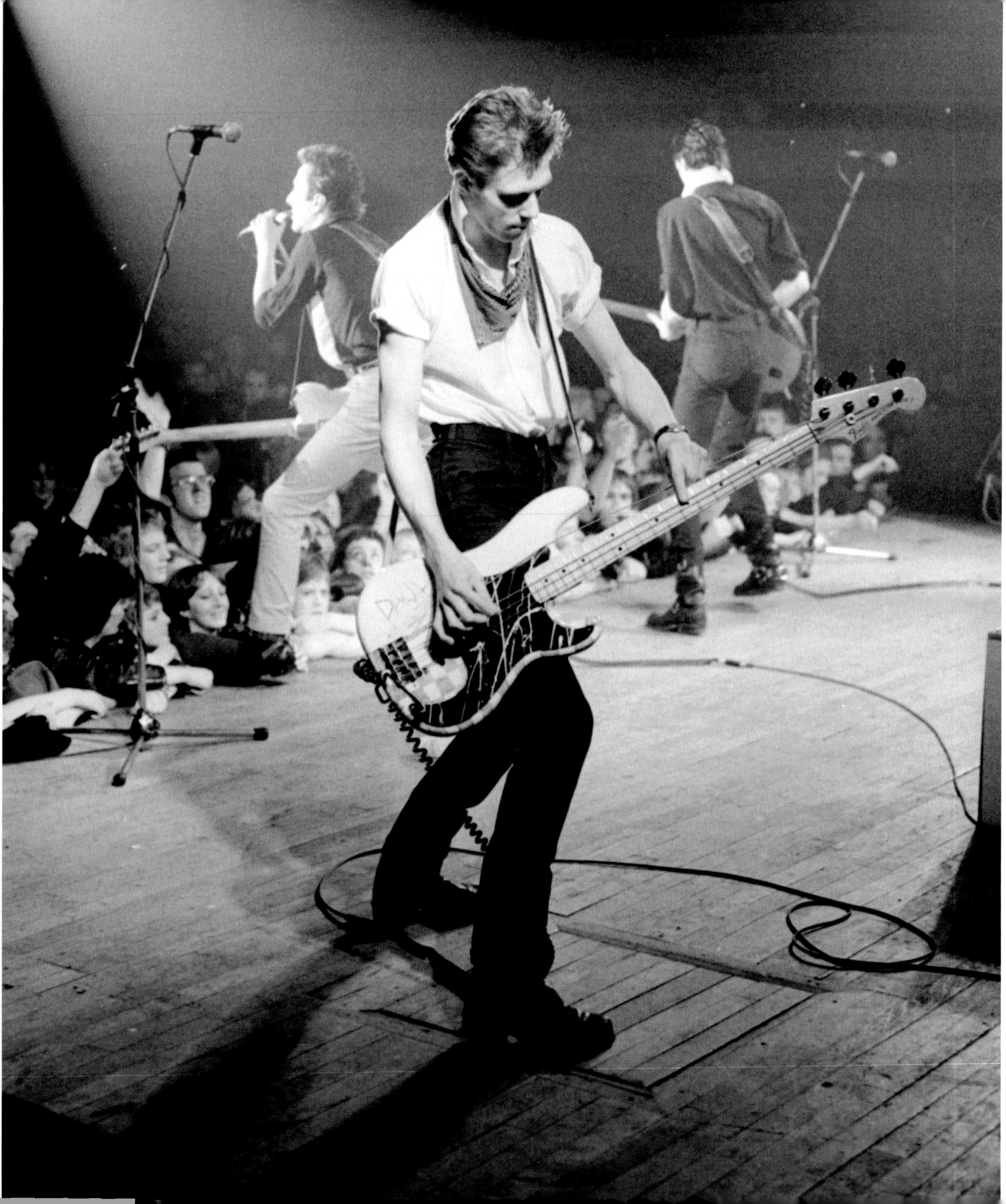

DECEMBER

THE CLASH'S CALLING CARD

The Clash's every move was scrutinized, discussed and judged. After all they were 'the only band that mattered'. The verdict was not always favourable however and, in the summer of 1979, the band were at a crossroads, needing to prove themselves again. Produced by the maverick Guy Stevens, LONDON CALLING was a triumph from the iconic guitar-smashing cover to the 19 songs spread over four sides of vinyl. It was released in the UK on 14 December 1979. The music shattered the orthodoxies of punk, taking in rockabilly, jazz and pop. Beginning with the apocalyptic call to arms of the title track and culminating in the soul-influenced 'Train In Vain' (not listed on original copies), it was an instant classic.

1980

THE PISTOLS ON FILM

Polish-American director Lech Kowalski based his punk documentary, *D.O.A: A Rite of Passage*, around The Sex Pistols' American 1978 tour, which ended in the band's dissolution. Footage from the tour was intercut with live performances by other British punk bands, Generation X, The Dead Boys, Rich Kids, X-Ray Spex and Sham 69. Iggy Pop and The Clash also feature. Along with the music there are interviews, the most notorious of which is with Sid Vicious and Nancy Spungen; Sid repeatedly nods off mid-interview. The grainy, hand-held filming makes for a suitably edgy atmosphere and the live footage provides an invaluable record of early punk.

FEBRUARY

THE RAMONES' END OF THE CENTURY

Their appearance in the movie ROCK'N'ROLL HIGH SCHOOL brought The Ramones to the attention of legendary wall-of-sound originator Phil Spector, who produced END OF THE CENTURY, their fifth album. The match was far from perfect as the notoriously demanding Spector required multiple takes in the studio and, according to bassist Dee Dee Ramone, demonstrated his fondness for firearms by holding the band hostage at gunpoint during the sessions. END OF THE CENTURY, released on 4 February 1980, was The Ramones' most successful album, reaching No. 44 on the *Billboard* chart and No. 14 in the UK charts, where it spawned a Top 10 single, the band's cover of Spector's 'Baby I Love You'.

APRIL

X'S LOS ANGELES

X were among the first punk bands to form in Los Angeles in 1977. The line-up comprised female singer Exene Cervenka, bassist John Doe, guitarist Billy Zoom and drummer DJ Bonebrake. After two independent singles, the band released their debut album LOS ANGELES on 26 April 1980. Clocking in at less than half an hour, the album is regarded as a seminal American punk record. It was produced by Doors' keyboard player Ray Manzarek, as was X's second album WILD GIFT, which was voted album of the year in 1981 by *The Los Angeles Times* and *The New York Times*.

MAY

THE DEAD KENNEDYS ON HOLIDAY

The Dead Kennedys' second single, 'Holiday In Cambodia' released in May 1980, continued where their first left off, with a typically visceral performance and a characteristically politicized lyric. Frontman Jello Biafra turned his satirical eye to liberal rich American college students, whose supposedly enlightened beliefs are at odds with their complacent indifference to the anguish caused by their country's foreign policy in places like Cambodia. The song became a bone of contention between band members when the ex-members sued Biafra for unpaid royalties after his refusal to license its use in a Levi's jeans commercial.

July

JOY DIVISION'S CLOSER

Recorded in March 1980, the second Joy Division album had a richer sound with more emphasis on keyboards and synthesizer. The stately, elegiac and sometimes funereal feel to *CLOSER*, and the tomb depicted on the cover, took on tragic proportions following the suicide of singer Ian Curtis in May 1980, shortly before Joy Division's first US tour. Beset by worsening epilepsy and haunted by the collapse of his marriage, Curtis had already made one attempt on his life before hanging himself in his Macclesfield home. The album was released on 18 July 1980 to universal acclaim and Joy Division passed into legend, inspiring two feature films.

AUGUST

DEVO WHIP IT UP

Hailing from Akron, Ohio, America's rubber capital, Devo was formed by students at Kent State University. Their name referred to the notion that mankind was devolving rather than progressing. That notion informed their early recordings, including their debut album, the Brian Eno produced **Q: ARE WE NOT MEN? A: WE ARE DEVO!** Taken from third album **FREEDOM OF CHOICE**, 'Whip It!', released as a single in August 1980, was their only US Top 40 hit. The song was helped on its way by a striking video featuring singer Mark Mothersbaugh whipping the clothes off a woman. The video went on to receive heavy airplay when MTV was launched the following year.

SEPTEMBER

THE DEAD KENNEDYS' FRUIT AND VEGETABLES

The 14 songs on **FRESH FRUIT FOR ROTTING VEGETABLES** were laid down live in the studio by The Dead Kennedys; overdubs were kept to a minimum. The album, which was originally released on 2 September 1980, stuck to the blueprint established on the band's first two singles, re-recorded versions of which appear on it. Likewise, Jello Biafra's incendiary political lyrics are a defining feature: titles like 'When Ya Get Drafted', 'Chemical Warfare' and 'Let's Lynch The Landlord' tell their own story. The album closed with a sarcastic cover of 'Viva Las Vegas'. The cover image of burning police cars drove the point home.

OCTOBER

MOTÖRHEAD'S ACE IN THE HOLE

Despite mutual hostility between the two sets of fans, the combination of heavy metal and punk was a sure-fire winner, and it fell to former Hawkwind bassist Lemmy to realize the vision. He put together his power trio in 1975 and they played suitably loud, hard and fast. 'Ace Of Spades' is perhaps the definitive Motörhead anthem with its dive-bomb riff and fatalistic gambling lyric. Lemmy sings like he has been gargling razor blades. Taken from their third album, also entitled ACE OF SPADES, the song was released as a single on 27 October 1980 and it put Motörhead back in the UK charts, peaking at No. 15.

DECEMBER

THE CLASH'S SANDINISTA!

SANDINISTA! saw The Clash leave punk and, in many ways, conventional rock behind them. The most divisive album of a career not short on controversy, SANDINISTA! was a sprawling three-record set clocking in at two and a half hours. Having recorded a surfeit of material during the course of 1980, the band elected to unleash it all at once on 12 December 1980. Listeners were delighted and confounded in equal measures by the cornucopia on offer. Ahead of its time in its all-embracing approach, SANDINISTA! embraced dub reggae, folk, blues, hip-hop – 'The Magnificent Seven' is the first example of white rap – rockabilly, calypso, soul and gospel.

1981

FEBRUARY

TALKING HEADS' 'ONCE IN A LIFETIME'

With its African-inspired rhythm conflicting with the rhythm played
by the band, 'Once In A Lifetime' made for an unlikely hit single
for Talking Heads. Although it failed to dent the American chart,
the song made more impact in Britain where it reached No. 14.
Much of its success was due to an innovative video, which
featured Heads' leader David Byrne's ungainly dancing style. The
clip became a staple of early MTV. 'Once In A Lifetime', released
on 2 February 1981, was taken from the band's fourth album
REMAIN IN LIGHT, which saw them continue to develop beyond
the confines of new wave rock.

July

THE Oi SCENE

A peculiarly British offshoot of punk, Oi was meant to return the music to the working classes with a style that combined energy with terrace chant choruses. Its leading exponents were The 4-Skins, Angelic Upstarts, The Exploited and Cockney Rejects (pictured opposite). The last were standard-bearers for the scene, with their song 'Oi, Oi, Oi' giving the movement its name. In 1980, The Rejects' single 'The Greatest Cockney Rip-Off' was a UK Top 30 hit. Subsequently, Oi became associated with fascist and racist politics and the firebombing by Asians of a gig in Southall on 4 July 1981 spelled the beginning of the end.

ANARCHO-PUNK IN THE UK

Anarchy had been associated with punk rock since the release of The Sex Pistols' debut single, although the term was often used as a slogan with little real understanding of the political theory behind it. Formed in 1977 at a London commune, Crass (pictured above) were instrumental in creating the sub-genre known as anarcho-punk, which developed alongside hardcore in the States and Oi in Britain. The scene grew to embrace Poison Girls, A Flux Of Pink Indians, Subhumans, Conflict and The Apostles. Anarcho-punk mutated into grindcore in the mid-1980s, but Crass remained true to its original ideology.

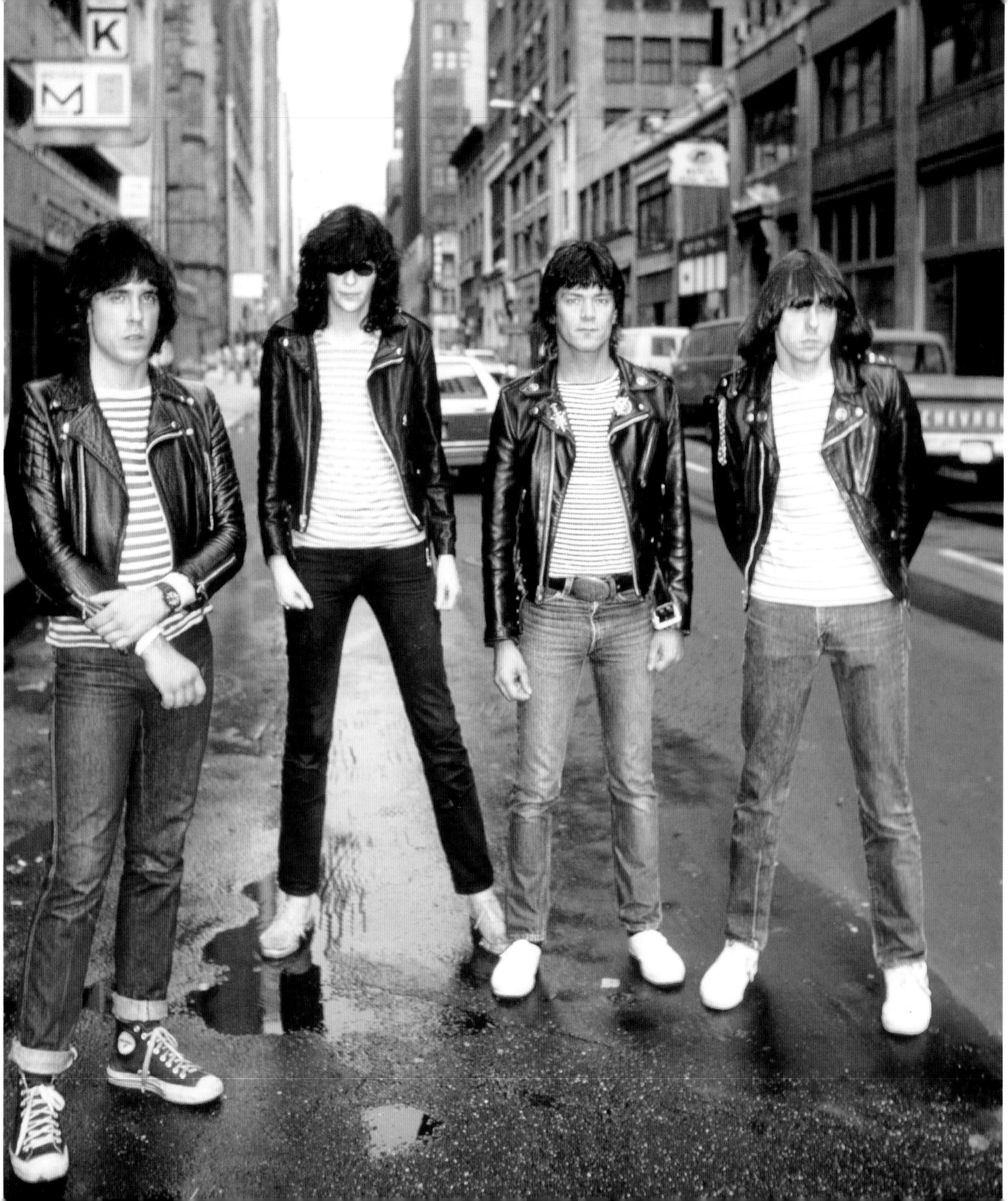
K

JULY

THE RAMONES' PLEASANT DREAMS

The sixth Ramones album, **PLEASANT DREAMS**, released on 20 July 1981, was a different affair to its predecessor, but fell short of returning the band to their punk roots. Instead, The Ramones developed a sound that was condemned by singer Joey Ramone as too slick. The producer was former 10cc man Graham Gouldman, whose brief from the record company was to give The Ramones a more radio-friendly heavy metal sheen. There were no covers, the songs were all written by either Joey or Dee Dee Ramone. Joey's lyrics frequently refer to guitarist Johnny Ramone stealing his girlfriend and the tension caused by that.

DECEMBER

BLACK FLAG GO HARDCORE

One of the first punk outfits on America's West Coast, Black Flag went on to become pioneers of hardcore. The Californians recruited fan and sometime roadie Henry Rollins as lead vocalist shortly before recording **DAMAGED**, their debut album. When major label MCA baulked at the content, Black Flag released it on their own imprint on 5 December 1981. Very much an underground classic at the time, the album's reputation has since grown to the extent that it is now fêted as a punk landmark. The guitars were recorded live without separation and Rollins' vocals were added later. The deliberately lo-fi production captures Black Flag at their peak.

1982

HARDCORE RAGES ON

In the wake of Black Flag, the style that would be christened hardcore began to coalesce in Los Angeles, with corresponding scenes on the East Coast, Washington DC and Boston, whilst The Dead Kennedys operated out of San Francisco. Hardcore emphasizes rhythm over melody, overlaid with impassioned, screaming vocals. Along with the originators of the movement, important bands include The Germs (pictured above), Fear, Middle Class, Big Boys, Bad Brains and Misfits. Although they only made one album, The Germs are fondly remembered; many years later guitarist Pat Smear worked with Nirvana and Foo Fighters.

THE NO WAVE SCENE

Whilst hardcore emerged from the visceral side of punk, no wave owed its origins to its artier aspects. As a musical style, no wave was hard to define as it drew on various genres, but a driving rhythm and a certain atonal quality were key. The scene began in New York, the traditional home of art-punk. The movement was short-lived, its most enduring graduates being experimental rockers Sonic Youth. Saxophonist James Chance and writer/singer/poet Lydia Lunch (pictured opposite) were two central figures, forming the band Teenage Jesus & The Jerks, although Chance swiftly left to found The Contortions.

MAY

THE CLASH'S COMBAT ROCK AND BEYOND

COMBAT ROCK was pared down by producer Glyn Johns to a single album from a double prepared by guitarist Mick Jones. The experimentation of SANDINISTA! continued with further forays into hip-hop and a spoken-word contribution from legendary beat poet Allen Ginsberg. It was The Clash's commercial peak, reaching No. 2 in the UK and cracking the Top 10 in America. 'Rock The Casbah' was the band's biggest hit single until the posthumous UK No. 1 'Should I Stay Or Should I Go?'. The Clash started to disintegrate soon after COMBAT ROCK, which was released on 14 May 1982. CUT THE CRAP, made after Jones and drummer Topper Headon had been fired, was released in 1985 but has since been expunged from the canon.

1983

FEBRUARY

THE REMAINS OF THE RAMONES

After the detours of the previous two albums, SUBTERRANEAN JUNGLE, released on 28 February 1983, was welcomed as something of a return to what The Ramones did best, if not exactly a return to vintage form. Producers Ritchie Cordell and Glen Kolotkin, heads of the power-pop and punk label Bomp!, were credited with getting The Ramones back on track. On 'Time Bomb' Dee Dee Ramone enjoys his first lead vocal on a Ramones album. The sessions saw the dismissal of drummer Marky Ramone because of alcoholism. SUBTERRANEAN JUNGLE set the template for the rest of the band's career and was their last album to reach the *Billboard* chart.

MARCH

POST-PUNK CROSSES OVER

A term coined by the British music press, post-punk was used to describe a variety of disparate artists, from those originally associated with punk, like Siouxsie & The Banshees, to those galvanized by it, like XTC. The most successful post-punk bands added a commercial edge to their music and entered the mainstream. Emerging from the ashes of Joy Division, New Order (pictured opposite) blended rock and dance rhythms to become one of the most important bands of the 1980s and 1990s. Their hit single 'Blue Monday', released on 7 March 1983, became the UK's biggest-selling 12-inch single of all time. Meanwhile, The Cure's atmospheric gothic rock earned them large audiences in both Britain and America.

EPILOGUE

PUNK TURNS POP

Perhaps the antidote to hardcore, punk-pop emphasizes melody and embraces traditional pop music topics such as love and relationships, yet is played with speed and energy. The early Ramones albums represented a prototype of the style, whilst British groups like The Jam, Buzzcocks and The Undertones can claim to have built on the foundations. The genre came of age in the mid-1990s when both Blink-182 and Green Day (pictured above) enjoyed massive success. Blink-182's fast-paced teen angst was hugely popular and Green Day's 1994 debut album DOOKIE was a crossover smash.

INDEX